The Non-League Foot
STAFFORDSHIRE &

by Colin Peel & Mick Blakeman

Photography by Colin Peel, except where indicated

Series Editor: Mike Floate   Designed by Colin Peel & Mike Floate   Series Consultant: Colin Peel

Published by Newlands Printing Services, Newlands Cottages, Stones Cross Road,
Crockenhill, Swanley, Kent BR8 8LX

© Colin Peel, Mick Blakeman & Mike Floate 2003

All rights reserved. No part of this publication may be reproduced or copied in any manner without the permission of the copyright holders. Considerable effort has been made to ensure the accuracy of information in this book, but things will inevitably change and the publisher or authors cannot accept responsibility for any consequences arising from the use of this book.

British Library Cataloguing in Publication Data.
A catalogue record for this volume is available from the British Library.

Photo above: The 'stone dominoes' at the ground of Stone Dominoes in Yarnfield. The dominoes spell out '1-9-8-7', the year of the club's formation.
Front Cover: Shrewsbury Town FC   Back cover: Newcastle FC

ISBN 1 900257 13 0

Printed and bound by Catford Print Centre (020-8695 0101)

Acknowledgements

Mick would like to thank the following for their help with the researches for this book:

From libraries and county archive services: The staff of the Staffordshire County Record Office in Stafford, Chris Copp at Staffordshire Archives and the staff of Shropshire Archives in Shrewsbury, particularly Tony Carr, Andrew Davidson and Edwin Hedges. The staff of Tamworth Castle Museum. The staff of the local studies sections of the libraries at Barton-under-Needwood, Burton-on-Trent, Cannock, Hanley, Hednesford, Leek, Lichfield, Rugeley, Tamworth, Telford and Whitchurch. The staff of Simmons Aerofilms in Potters Bar.

From the local media: John Harper and Rob Tanner of the Tamworth Herald, Rex Page of the Burton Mail, James Garrison and Paul James of the Shropshire Star, Dave Gregory and James Baylis of Partnership Publishing Limited and James Bond and Nigel Dolman of BBC Radio Shropshire.

Club officials: Mike Ferriday of Telford United, Peter Gwilliam of Ludlow Town and Fleur Robinson of Burton Albion.

The following individuals: Gordon Allcock, Jim Barmbrook, Reg Barnsley, Mr. S. Bennett, Mr. C. Birch, John Bradbury, Derek Burt, Max Chadwick, Jim Cooper, Lou Edwards, Mark Guryn, Pete Haynes, Tim Hebbard, Zoe Holt, Mr. C. Kelly, Ray Millership, Bert Morris, Brian Morris, Roy Pearce, Gary Pegg, Paul Quinn, Dave Rymer, Keith Stanley, Mabel Swift, Geoff Taverner, Mr. G. Vater, Malcolm Ward, Ben Whittle, Terry Wilding, Mrs. Williams and Harry Wilshaw.

Colin would like to thank Bob Lilliman and Andy Dakin for access to their comprehensive photographic archives, and the following people for their help: Bill Berry, Brian Cook, Leo Hoenig, Tim Grose, Vince Taylor and Dean Walton. He would also like to credit his own decision to involve Mick Blakeman in the research and authoring of the book.

Key Sources: Listing every reference work used in the compilation of the book would be unrealistic, but the authors would like to credit the following sources in particular:

Richard Rundle's Football Club History Database (www.fchd.btinternet.com)
'The Non-League Club Directories' edited by Tony Williams between 1978 and 2002
'The History of Cheddleton Mental Hospital' by Max Chadwick and David Pearson
'The History of non-League Football Grounds' by Kerry Miller
'The non-League Football Grounds of Great Britain' edited by Tony Williams
The mapping resources of www.multimap.com, the Geographers' A-Z Map Company, and the Ordnance Survey.

Left: Cannock Sports Stadium

Introduction

The adjoining counties of Staffordshire and Shropshire have a rich diversity of non-League football grounds. The top of the pyramid is represented by four Conference grounds while there is at least one ground at every level down to the county leagues some six rungs below. There are also notable grounds that fall outside the pyramid for various reasons such as the current use being for ladies' football, Sunday football or as training facilities.

The book describes almost every ground currently staging football down to County League level, and every past ground that provided proper facilities for spectators, such as cover or terracing. Generally speaking, the more there is to describe, the more space is given to that ground. Even then, some significant clubs have played on grounds that were just fields with goalposts and so these have been included to avoid leaving any significant gaps in history.

The authors have worked closely together on the book with Colin taking responsibility for describing most of the present grounds and Mick most of the past grounds. One or the other of us – and often both – have visited every ground described, even those that have disappeared under housing developments. We hoped to find at least one substantial ground whose existence was previously unknown to us and the fascinating discovery at the old Cheddleton Asylum fulfilled that ambition. We are also delighted to be publishing many rare and previously unseen photographs of long forgotten grounds.

We have also been fortunate to see superb brand new developments such as those at Telford and Ludlow, historic old stands such as that at Burton rugby ground, curiosities such as the dominoes at Stone and sad relics such as those at Hanley and Chell. There are smart modern grounds like Hednesford, well established grounds like Stafford and long forgotten grounds like Cannock Town. There are town centre grounds like Shrewsbury and beautiful countryside grounds like Newcastle-on-Clun. The diversity is amazing, yet one thing is common – whether in Leek or Ludlow, in Tamworth or Telford – and that is the kindness and courtesy of the people we have asked for help, be they club officials, library staff, working for the local press or local radio, or simply fans like us.

Colin Peel
Mick Blakeman
November 2003

Below:
Foley F.C.

Burton Albion F.C.

Eton Park, Princess Way,
Burton-on-Trent DE14 2RU
01283-565938

Burton Albion have invested heavily enough in Eton Park to acquire a Conference grading but if their attempt to gain planning permission for a new ground is successful then the club will soon be on the move for the third time in its relatively short history.

The Brewers want to build a 6,000-capacity stadium directly to the north of Eton Park on land currently occupied by the Pirelli Sports Ground, and if everything goes according to plan then the move could take place as early as the 2004/05 season.

Since opening in September 1958, Eton Park has evolved and improved steadily rather than spectacularly. The 1960s Grandstand, elevated above the changing rooms and covered with a forward-sloping roof, had its benches changed for orange plastic seats in the late 1980s. Albion needed more seats to enter the Conference so a very tidy extension was built in a matching style during 2001 to take the number of seats up to 640, one of which has regularly been occupied by the great Brian Clough during his son Nigel's successful reign as player-manager.

Looking from the stand, the Brook End terrace is to the left. This was originally a cinder bank but is now properly terraced with the original roof still surviving. Behind the terrace is a 300-space car park, and this end also houses the club shop. Opposite is the Popular Side terrace, built during the 1960s with a long, low, plain roof that requires over twenty pillars to support it. Away to the right is the Gordon Bray terrace, built in the mid 1990s over what was originally a grass bank with a few crush barriers scattered around. This is a particularly solid construction, but once again it is impossible to get an unobstructed view because of a forest of roof supports placed along the front. This is one aspect of watching football in Burton that would be greatly enhanced by the use of modern construction techniques on the new ground.

Burton Albion F.C.

Eton Park is on its third set of floodlights. The first set, acquired from Bristol City in 1965, was mounted on fourteen pylons, seven on each side of the pitch. This meant that patrons of the Popular Side terrace would have been faced with over thirty obstructions to a clear view!

Thankfully, a new set of lights mounted on pylons in each corner arrived in the late 1980s, and these have since been replaced by ultra-modern slim pylons.

First-time visitors cannot fail to note how cheerful all the stands look thanks to the gallons of yellow and black paint that cover just about every surface.

Eton Park will be sadly missed if the Brewers manage to trade up to a new stadium. The ground has seen FA Trophy Semi-Finals, great FA Cup matches and promotion to the highest level of non-League. Yet the club's destiny is to put the famous old town back on the map of the Football League, and if a new stadium is what it takes, then so be it.

Above top: The Brook End terrace in 1978 (pic: Bob Lilliman). **Above middle**: The grassed South end in the early 90s (pic: Andy Dakin). **Above bottom**: The Gordon Bray terrace. **Left**: Eton Park's lofty Grandstand in 1978 (pic: Bob Lilliman). **Below**: The new extended Grandstand.

Hednesford Town F.C.

Keys Park, Hill Street,
Hednesford, WS12 2DZ
01543-422870

Looking around the model development that is Keys Park, it is difficult to believe that less than a decade ago Hednesford Town were playing at the ramshackle, antiquated ground behind the Cross Keys pub just a few yards up the road. The move was like swapping a moth-eaten, saggy and well-loved old armchair for a plush, modern sofa from Ikea, yet the ambition of the people running the club at the time was quickly rewarded as Hednesford were able to inaugurate Keys Park as a newly-promoted Conference side.

What is particularly impressive, though, is that Hednesford Town have kept good their promises to enlarge the ground from its original state to one that is acceptable to the Football League, achieving this despite relegation from the Conference in 2001. It is, as they say, a lot of ground for such a small place.

Keys Park opened in August 1995 on the site of a former brickworks less than half a mile south of the Cross Keys ground, which is now housing. The Main Stand, just about the only part of the ground not to have changed since 1995, is built as an extension from the large clubhouse building. The tall roof cantilevers over some 700 sharply-raked seats with the help of angled struts. At the back of the stand, windows from a range of suites and function rooms look out onto the pitch. It is also clear to see that if the Pitmen needed to add more seats, they could extend the stand on either side and treble the number. Behind the stand is a massive car park.

Top: Keys Park in 1995
Below: ...and 2002

Hednesford Town F.C.

At the North, or Hednesford End seats were placed under the original roof and this became used for away fans when segregation was in force. This brought the total number of seats in Keys Park to a substantial 1,025.

Meanwhile, the South, or Heath Hayes End was also rebuilt and re-roofed to roughly double the height of the original terrace. Finally, the East Terrace, by now known as the Wimblebury Terrace acquired a cantilever roof along its full length even though the club had been relegated back to the Dr Martens League.

This was the last phase in the development of Keys Park to Football League standard as the total capacity passed the magic 6,000 figure by a number of 500. Hednesford are one of those clubs that must have heaved a sigh of exasperation at the news in 2003 that as part of a deal to divert funds from the Football Foundation to cash-strapped Football League clubs, a ground capacity of 4,500 would be the new minimum for joining the League.

Still, it's early days for Keys Park and if the Pitmen do get another whiff of the big-time, they will have the room and facilities to house large crowds in comfort. That is something they could never do at the old place.

Leek Town F.C.

Harrison Park, Macclesfield Road,
Leek ST13 8LD
01538-399278

What makes Harrison Park greater than the sum of its parts is the strong sense of enclosure provided by the surroundings. Three sides of this quintessentially Northern ground feature fairly basic covered terracing, whilst the fourth has a collection of random outbuildings alongside an admittedly magnificent grandstand, but throw in the setting – part industrial, part residential, part scenic – and the result is a truly atmospheric little ground that is one of non-League's best.

Leek's home developed gradually alongside the fortunes of the club. By the time of Leek's entry into the Cheshire County League in 1973, the homely little stand had the floodlights from Rugby Town's old ground for company – the pylons are still in service but with rather newer bulbs. The club' rise through the pyramid to the Northern Premier League saw the ground fully enclosed and covered terracing built on all three sides. In 1992 the club began to prepare the ground for Conference football by demolishing the old stand and building a lofty replacement that would come to dominate the ground. When Leek finally were allowed into the Conference in 1997, their stay lasted an all-too-brief two seasons, and a further relegation in 2001 sees them back in the lower division of the Northern Premier. The ground has been shared by North-West Counties League side Leek CSOB for well over a decade.

Sited just off the town centre on the main road to Macclesfield, there is only a small amount of parking, so it's a case of finding a space in the town itself or on the main road. To get the best view of the ground, a climb up the bank behind the south goal is highly recommended.

Leek Town F.C.

This can be accessed from the car park or from Kiln Lane, a narrow road that runs up the hill. Although some cunningly planted trees are gradually eroding the free view of the match from the bank, the view is still superb. A factory building on the other side of the main road looms behind the far goal, and to the left of here is a chemical works. It all looks slightly incongruous against the verdant backdrop of the rolling Staffordshire moorlands.

To the left as you look from the bank, the 500-seat Grandstand occupies about fifty yards of touchline towards the south goal. The seating deck is perched above a paddock terrace, which shows how the club had to maximise the space in the ground to arrive at a capacity of 3,500. The stand has a cantilevered roof which is nicely decked out in white cladding with blue trimmings, but the fact that blue steelwork was also used only becomes apparent once you are beneath the roof.

The terracing at each end is shallow and covered along the full length with low roofing. The Town Side terracing is looking a little faded and is an area of the ground that Leek have the potential to improve by relaying the concrete. Behind this side is a row of houses to complete the impression of a ground that is so hemmed in that despite the competing attractions of the scenery all attention is drawn to the pitch, which is how it should be.

Above: Leek Town's original stand in 1978 (pic: Bob Lilliman).
Below: The new stand nearing completion in 1992 (pic: Andy Dakin).
Bottom: The east terrace.

NON-LEAGUE GROUNDS ● 9 ● STAFFORDSHIRE & SHROPSHIRE

Shrewsbury Town F.C.
Gay Meadow, Abbey Foregate,
Shrewsbury SY2 6AB
01743-360111

That Gay Meadow is even in a book about non-League grounds is difficult to comprehend, but it is a most welcome inclusion. For all the problems that come with a flood-prone site in an ancient town centre, Gay Meadow is one of our most celebrated football grounds, a place you would take a foreign visitor to explain the attractions of English football away from the hype and hassle of the Premiership.

Sadly, with its Centenary as a football ground due in 2010, time is running out for Gay Meadow. The catastrophic floods of October 1998 made the club more determined than ever to relocate to Meole Brace and a site in Oteley Road, not far from the A5, where space exists for a modern 10,000-seat stadium. Even die-hard fans of Shrewsbury have come to accept the inevitability of a move away from a home which is routinely – and justifiably – described as 'charming' and 'idyllic'. At least there will be no major works at the ground until the move takes place, so there is still time to enjoy one of the jewels of English football in a relatively unspoilt state.

Gay Meadow is reached via a narrow road off the one-way Abbey Foregate. There is a fair-sized car park at the ground but a better option is to park up by one of the main roads leading to the A5 and walk to the ground. Those arriving at the station have the pleasure of a stroll through the town to reach the ground.

Another reason for the club wanting to move is restricted access to half the ground. The recently extended Wakeman School is right up against the south terrace, (the Wakeman End), and the west terrace backs onto the River Severn, so all the entrances are grouped around the car park. Going through the turnstiles to the left of the Grandstand leads onto the south terrace, where it is only natural to pause and take in the majestic scene in front of you.

Shrewsbury Town F.C.

The open Wakeman End is quite narrow but, since the removal of the obtrusive fencing from the front, the view is fine. The terrace is overlooked by the school and a line of trees. You have to walk past this end to reach the Riverside Terrace, which has quite a shallow gradient and plenty of crush barriers. The roof is slightly cranked and held up by eighteen supports along the front, with a line of advertising boards tucked beneath the lip. The backdrop to this side is stunning; tall trees lie between the terrace and the river, and the town rises on the far bank, with the spire of St Mary's prominent.

What makes Gay Meadow so attractive is the way that the ground is beautifully framed by the school, the trees, the town and the classic 1959 floodlights mounted on lattice-work towers in each corner.

To the north is the Station End, another terrace which is quite deep but shallow. The rear half has a basic cover and the presence of away fans at this end accounts for the survival of a perimeter fence. Finally, there is the 4,000-seat stand, which appears as one entity but is divided into three sections according to the construction date of each part: 1922 (Centre), 1938 (Station) and 1966 (Wakeman). The latter section has a clashing roof-style but a slightly better view.

Capacity is down to 8,000 from a record crowd of 18,917 set in 1961. It is not hard to envisage such large crowds at Gay Meadow. For a start, today's crowd of 8,000 is not excessively cramped. Back then, there was more terracing, fewer aisles, no segregation and, as my co-author (who was there at the time) grimly noted, "no-one ever tried to reach the toilets."

<u>Glorious Gay Meadow. Top</u>: The Wakeman End. **Middle**: The Riverside Terrace. **Bottom**: The multi-section stand and a proper pair of stanchions.

NON-LEAGUE GROUNDS • 11 • STAFFORDSHIRE & SHROPSHIRE

Stafford Rangers F.C.

Marston Road, Stafford
ST16 3BX
01785-602430

Marston Road was surprisingly basic until the mid-1970s, when both club and ground went through a purple patch. Victorious in two out of three visits to Wembley in the FA Trophy Final, the decade finished with Stafford becoming founder members of the Alliance Premier League (now Conference). Since then the fortunes of the club have ebbed and flowed somewhat, and the only substantial development at the ground since Rangers left the Conference in 1995 has been to build over part of the terracing at one end. In tidal terms, however, it would seem that Rangers are back on a flow, so ground improvements could be on the agenda in the near future.

The early 1920s was a formative period for the ground, as Rangers built a low stand on the Marston Road side and a fifty-yard stretch of covered terracing opposite. Not much changed until after WW2, when the cover on the east side was extended towards the Town End. The middle section of the Town End terrace was itself covered in the 1950s.

Above: Marston Road in 1969 before the industrial estate was built over the second pitch (pic: Aerofilms A195386).
Below: The ground in 2003.

Stafford Rangers F.C.

It is strange to think that the record crowd of 8,536 (for an FA Cup match in January 1975) was set with the old stand still in place, but by the start of the 1975/76 season a tall new cantilever stand was ready for occupation. This provides 426 seats and is currently sponsored by a well-known lager brand.

The mid-1970s also saw an industrial estate built over the pitch that lay to the north of the ground, and the establishment of an impressive clubhouse and changing facility in the north-west corner. The main entrance moved from Marston Road to the newly-built Astonfields Road, where a car park was also provided.

On entering the ground, the north end of the ground seems quite busy, partly because the terrace behind the goal has been severely reduced by the building of an indoor sports hall. To the right is the stand, which hardly seems to have aged in the nigh-on thirty years of service, a club shop and refreshment areas. To the left is the original 1922 cover, which has been kept in excellent condition by the club. The newer section can be clearly seen despite being over fifty years old. The Town End is a spacious terrace with a fairly functional roof in the centre which has also been well looked-after.

Marston Road has an overwhelming sense of space created by the deepness of the terrace steps as well as some

Top: The old stand in March 1972 (pic: Bob Lilliman). *Middle*: The 1975 replacement stand, which could hardly be more different. *Bottom*: The covered terrace on the east side.

underused areas of the ground. The team is on a mission to recapture the glory of the seventies, but it could be that Marston Road's best days are yet to come.

Tamworth F.C.

The Lamb Ground, Kettlebrook Road,
Tamworth B77 1AA
01827-65798

What The Lamb lacks in grandeur it more than makes up for in atmosphere. A decent sized crowd in this ground can make the stands seem twice as tall and the slope twice as steep to any visiting team that isn't prepared to do battle. It's a purist's delight.

Tamworth have realised the limitations of the site however, and have decided that their future will be best served by a move to a purpose-built new stadium capable of expansion to 7,000 capacity. There are several hurdles to clear before any move can take place, so it's likely that The Lamb will be in service for at least a few more seasons.

The original stand was a long low affair dating from the late 1940s. Built facing into the sun on the north side of the ground, the fascia was deep and the view blocked by twelve roof supports. Around the same time the 'Shed' terrace was built on the opposite side and apart from the installation of floodlights in 1969 not much changed at The Lamb until the 1990s.

*Above: The Lamb in 1988 seen from the grassed Castle End. **This picture**: The same view in 2003*

Tamworth F.C.

Firstly, the Meadow Street End at the top of the ground was properly terraced and given a roof to match the much older Shed terrace. The major changes happened in the Summer of 1996, when the old stand made way for a modern cantilevered stand seating 426. At the Castle End of the ground, the grass banking that ran all the way to the perimeter fence was properly terraced at the front and a new road constructed behind the terracing to lead from the main car park to the clubhouse. Further upgrades to non-spectator areas equipped The Lamb for the Conference, which they finally joined in 2003.

The ground's location is an obvious attraction to potential developers, especially if access could be opened onto the 'Tamworth Egg', a system of roundabouts on the town's ring road. As things stand, the ground is accessed via a narrow entrance off Kettlebrook Road, which leads onto a vast car park. It's this car park which borders onto the ring road.

Gates at the far end lead to the Castle End, which used to be a grass bank but is now a five-step terrace. To the left is the modern stand, whose clean lines are embellished by red trimmings and a club crest placed on a centre gable. The new stand would be resited at the new ground if the club does move. The end-to-end slope is quite pronounced, running up towards the Meadow Street End, a narrow terrace split into pens by brickwork dividers; this end is given over to away fans if segregation is used. In the bottom right corner is a network of buildings housing the clubhouse, changing rooms, shop and tea bar. Finally,

Above: The old Grandstand (photo: Andy Dakin).
Below: The replacement Grandstand

Above: 'The Shed'.
Below: Meadow St End

there is 'The Shed', a stretch of terracing covered by a low red-painted roof. As the club website puts it, "The Shed has become home to a number of the club's more vociferous supporters. The atmosphere in the Shed can be very lively." Let's hope that this also moves to the new ground.

Telford United F.C.

New Bucks Head Stadium,
Watling Street, Wellington TF1 2NJ
01952-640064

The New Bucks Head Stadium is the result of probably the largest ever single facilities investment in non-League football. A reported outlay of £14m has given Telford United the best, if not the biggest, ground in the Conference. You will find a full history and photographs of the 'Old' Bucks Head towards the back of this book in the old grounds section – barely any of it survived the rebuild.

The amazing transformation began when millionaire property developer Andy Shaw took over the club in the late 1990s. The first redevelopment plans, announced in October 1998, envisaged the retention of the controversial East Stand, but the following Summer revised plans showed a completely rebuilt ground alongside a hotel, conference and residential complex.

Work began in the Summer of 2000, when Bucks Head was demolished and completely cleared, forcing the team to use Worcester City for their early home games. The North Terrace was the first part of the new ground to be completed, quickly followed by the East Terrace, which had a temporary shelter for press and officials, and a superb control room. The visit of Dagenham in October 2000 saw the return of action to Bucks Head as 2,371 crammed onto the two terraces. The South terrace opened in January 2001, taking capacity to 4,300 but there was still a gap where the West Stand was to go, and this gap remained until the Summer of 2002.

Right: The North End is first to appear in Summer 2000 (pic: Mick Blakeman). **Below**: January 2001 and a space where the West Stand will go. **Below right**: The finished West Stand seen from the same spot.

Telford United F.C.

Work began on the new West Stand, only to cease again when it was around a third complete. Construction of the 90-bed hotel also got underway and a frantic Summer of 2003 saw the West Stand finished and the ground ready to host Telford's 1000th match in the Conference on August 12th, 2003. The efforts of the club and the workers were rewarded when a crowd of 2,800 – the Bucks' largest ever crowd for a home Conference match – saw the 2-0 win over Exeter.

Above: The temporary East Stand in Jan 2001. *Below*: The Frank Nagington Stand in Aug 2003.

The Bucks Head pub, which lends its name to the ground, is still standing in the south-east corner. Further up Haybridge Road is the entrance to a large new car park which backs onto the north end. The modernity of the place is evident from the curtain-walling that covers the outside walls.

The turnstiles of the North Terrace, now named the David Hutchison Stand, lead onto a wide concourse with a bar, snack bar, TVs and even wall-mounted convection heaters. This is a level of comfort not found at many Football League venues, never mind the Conference. The terrace is home to United's more vocal support and features a high, arching roof that cantilevers out from the concourse.

From here, the open East Terrace is to the left along with new perspex dugouts. At the far end is the Frank Nagington Stand, identical to the North Terrace in almost every detail and used to house away fans. The new hotel abuts into the south-west corner with hospitality rooms overlooking the pitch. To the right is the new Sir Stephen Roberts (West) Stand, which provides 2,200 seats in a total capacity of 6,700. Like everything else in the ground, the stand is finished to a high quality, and the rake of the seats is unusually steep for a single-tier stand. The control box is perched on stilts in the north-west corner. Maybe the occupants will soon see Telford United make a start on a thousand matches in the Football League.

Above: The David Hutchison Stand.
Below: The new West Stand.

Biddulph Victoria F.C.
Tunstall Road, Knypersley,
Stoke-on-Trent ST8 7AQ
01782-522737

Still better known by their previous sobriquet of Knypersley Victoria, Biddulph have established their ground in a corner of a sports area dominated by a fine cricket oval. The cost of divorcing the pitch from cricketing territory is limited space on two sides of the ground and a stand which is set behind the goal.

The arrangement looks quite tidy, however, particularly after you've marched across the cricket pitch into an adjacent field, where an elevated view of the Vics' ground can be had. The floodlights, mounted on industrial-style pylons in each corner, help to define the ground, as does the new £70,000 all-weather training area behind the east goal.

The stand is a fairly basic, but high affair that first appeared in 1978. Twelve years later it was doubled in width and acquired seating for 200. Obviously, the presence of cricket at the venue is going to place constraints on future development, but many other clubs have developed more than adequate grounds in similarly tight settings, and Biddulph could certainly join them.

The ground is shared by Vale Victoria of the Staffordshire County League.

Bolehall Swifts F.C.
Rene Road, Bolehall,
Tamworth B77 3NN
01827-62637

Too often these days clubs will 'upgrade' their facilities by purchasing prefabricated stands of uniform appearance whose lack of character is matched by lack of architectural merit. It is pleasing, therefore, to find two stands at a relatively unsung ground such as Rene Road which are not only different from each other but different from almost any other stand around the country.

Set on a 1950s housing estate just to the east of Tamworth town centre, the ground occupies a large site, with a fair amount of parking next to the clubhouse. With space on either side of the post & rail, the gently sloping pitch seems vast and suited to passing football.

The older of the two stands is on the north side of the pitch and looks as though it has been adapted from a driving range because it is divided into partitioned sections. The stand has a brick base and corrugated iron roof with a large awning to keep the sun out of your eyes. The painting of the club name on the roof is a nice touch. The stand at the far, eastern end of the ground is curiously tall, with solid screen ends and bench seating. This stand is painted yellow and green, and another prominent sign leaves you in no doubt as to where you are.

NON-LEAGUE GROUNDS ● 19 ● STAFFORDSHIRE & SHROPSHIRE

Bridgnorth Town F.C.

Crown Meadow, Innage Lane,
Bridgnorth WV16 4HJ
01746-762747

Bridgnorth gets more than its fair share of tourists, but disappointingly few of them make their way out of the town centre to Crown Meadow. The ground, set in a quiet area of 1960s housing, provides a calming alternative to the bustling town. That's providing you've managed to park your car a sensible distance away; Crown Meadow is not well endowed for drivers so you might consider arriving in style on the town's Severn Valley Steam Railway.

The 1979 clubhouse is set below the pitch, behind the bottom goal. The small concrete cover at this end was the only section of cover for the first ten years of Bridgnorth's Southern League tenure which began in 1983.

In 1993 Crown Meadow was drastically improved by the erection of a smart, sleek 250-seat stand on the west side of the pitch. The roof supports curve elegantly over three

rows of neat green seats in a smaller version of a construction style which is popular in Belgium and Holland.

The rest of the ground has flat standing set at varying heights above the pitch, which is cut into gentle banking which rises to a peak in the north-east corner. The close proximity of housing on two sides of the ground will place constraints on any future development but Crown Meadow is a well-maintained venue which will continue to improve with age. A lived-in look will suit it well.

Brocton F.C.

Cannock Sports Stadium,
Pye Green Rd, Cannock WS11 2RW
01543-571898

Brocton traded up to the Cannock Stadium in 2002, having previously used Stafford's municipal athletics stadium at Rowley Park (see p.46). Brocton's original home ground next to the Chetwynd Arms pub in the village itself, on the edge of Cannock Chase, has not been developed but still plays host to the reserve team (see p.49).

The site of the stadium was originally open land bisected by a tramway which linked Cannock Colliery to Huntington Wharf. The area was later used for allotments until the early post-war years, when the 'Festival Stadium' was laid out. The name presumably links to the 1951 Festival of Britain. The stadium originally had a cycling track running outside a cinder running surface. During the 1960s the stadium acquired a large pavilion building and a pitched-roof grandstand capable of seating around 300 people. In 1986, Steve Cram opened a new £300,000 synthetic track and the Festival Stadium name was dropped in favour of the current title. A more recent £500,000 upgrade to the stadium has seen the extensive terracing covered with six rows of blue and yellow seats. 504 of the seats are uncovered but the 260 towards the north end, in front of the pavilion, have been covered by a plain but very substantial roof. Floodlights were also added as part of the upgrade.

It is unusual for an athletics stadium that the cover has been provided at the start of the sprint lanes rather than the finish. This is one of those athletics venues that will be acceptable to most football fans despite the extra distance to the pitch. After all, what other solely-occupied ground in the Midland Combination can boast 764 seats?

Chasetown F.C.

The Scholars, Church Street,
Chasetown WS7 3QL
01543-682222

Now in its 21st season of staging football, The Scholars is one of the best kept grounds in the region and never fails to impress with its tidiness. Though it has come of age in the sense of time, you could say that the ground is still at a formative stage of its development and that the addition of a new stand or terracing would be welcome.

Chasetown moved here in 1983 in order to meet the requirements for the Premier Division of the West Midlands League. Paradoxically, Chasetown's previous ground at the Burntwood Recreation Centre (see page 61) had a splendid, if ageing, grandstand that any club at this level would have been proud of, whereas The Scholars did not have any seating until 1987. Sadly, it was the complete destruction by fire of the stand at the old ground in 1983 which hastened Chasetown's move.

The only access to The Scholars is from Church Street, where a decent-sized car park fronts an impressive clubhouse which has sustained the club ever since the move. The sole cover on the ground is a verandah-style extension to the clubhouse, housing around 120 wooden seats. The rake of the seats is rather shallow, and looking into the sun, so the view can be bettered from other vantage points.

The other three sides are attractively backed by dense forestation which will help keep out the noise from the new M6 Toll Motorway which runs nearby to the south. Behind the west goal is a large space which could be developed into a training area. The Scholars should be set for a long and illustrious history, unlike two other notable local sporting venues which have been reduced to rubble – the Norton Canes Greyhound Stadium, and the remarkable Chasewater Harness Racing Track, which boasted a colossal glass-fronted stand for 3,000, but lasted just 25 years.

Dudley United Girls & Ladies F.C.

Mile Flat Sports Ground, Wall Heath, Staffs DY6 0AU

When Handrahan Timbers disbanded at the end of the 2002/03 season, it seemed unlikely that such a well-equipped ground would be without a tenant for long. The identity of that new tenant, however, is something of a surprise – a club whose players are entirely female.

Dudley United field a large number of teams right across the age spectrum, with the senior team in the West Midlands (Ladies) League, so the acquisition of Mile Flat as a base is a massive step forward not just for Dudley United but for womens' football as a whole.

Mile Flat is a rural ground just a few hundred yards into Staffordshire, and was originally the home of Black Country Works team Richard Thomas & Baldwins, who played briefly in the Worcestershire (now Midland) Combination. Mike Handrahan took over the ground in the 1980s, installing a team bearing his company's name, and a series of improvements followed, starting with a new post & rail and two sections of cover backing on to the road side of the ground. These covers were later combined and moved south a few yards, and a tiny grandstand for about 25 people was built opposite.

More recently the ground was equipped with floodlights to allow the club to carry on in the top division of the Midland Combination, but the continuing financial drain of running a club at this level led to Mr Handrahan calling it a day. The Timbers last League match was against another club with an uncertain future – Massey Ferguson.

Hanford F.C.

Northwood Stadium, Keelings Road,
Hanley, Stoke-on-Trent ST1 6PA
01782-234400

It's not for me to say if there is much call for an international standard athletics track in Hanley, so it's just as well that the facility is very much in demand for football. Midland League side Hanford moved into the Northwood Stadium, just off Hanley town centre, after abandoning their vandal-hit ground at Trentmill Road. This stood next to the similarly afflicted home of Eastwood Hanley (see p.64) and had a small cover.

Northwood Stadium is undeniably impressive for this level of football. Entering the car park at the western end of the complex you get a panoramic view of the spacious site.

Attention is naturally drawn to the 750-seat grandstand to the right. This has a high roof because it cantilevers out from the main facilities block, and with Hanford's crowds you will be able to pick a seat wherever you like. Opposite the stand are two blocks of open terracing. As this book was going to print, it was announced that Stoke City Council had been given a large grant towards the £235,000 cost of replacing the athletics track. There must be a few international events coming up.

Heath Hayes F.C.
Coppice Colliery Ground,
Newlands Lane, Heath Hayes,
Cannock WS12 3HH

Despite the looming presence of Hednesford Town just up the road, Heath Hayes have dragged themselves out of junior football over the last twenty years or so, developing a splendid little ground in the process.

Established as the Welfare Sports Ground for the Coppice Colliery (which closed in 1964) the ground is entered via a winding track off Newlands Lane. Once you're through the gates, a scramble up the tall bank behind the rear goal is recommended, as the view of the ground and its surroundings is superb.

There is no access behind the goal at the far end of the pitch, and the side to the right, where the dugouts are located, is also quite constrained. Nearly all the facilities are on the north side of the pitch. Taking pride of place is a very solid stand built in the last couple of seasons. The seats are covered by a flat roof with a very unusual angled fascia.

Tucked away in the far corner is the original standing cover, a basic metal construction, and close to the entrance is a further section of cover containing seats, separated from the newer stand by a modern changing block. The clashing styles of the buildings on this side of the pitch give the impression of a club keen to develop their ground but happy to do it a seemingly haphazard fashion. A ground to keep an eye on.

Kidsgrove Athletic F.C.

Clough Hall, Hollinwood Road,
Kidsgrove, Stoke-on-Trent ST7 1BQ
01782-782412

On my first visit to Kidsgrove, a club official remarked that they "like to do something on the ground every year." This explains quite a lot – such as how Kidsgrove have been able to develop both the ground and the team without going into serious financial difficulty, and why the ground now has some six sections of cover together with all the paraphernalia needed to stage matches in the Unibond League.

Clough Hall is quite a confined site between a housing estate and a wooded area, so parking is very restricted. Early photos lend the ground a misleadingly rural aspect and although there is a fair amount of surrounding foliage, Clough Hall is firmly enclosed by a concrete fence.

The small forecourt leads on to the 'business' side of the ground, with the clubhouse and changing facilities behind the low seated stands. These are actually three stands which have been fused into one by shuffling sections of roof around. Some of the seats have come from Northwich Victoria's Drill Field ground. The other three sides are all flat standing with sections of blue metal cover in the centre of each; by the time you are reading this, Kidsgrove may have built up terracing inside some of them as part of their annual improvement of their main asset.

Top left: Clough Hall circa 1990 (pic: Andy Dakin)
Centre: The main stand
Bottom: The Sentinel Stand

Ludlow Town F.C.
Coors Stadium, Bromfield Road,
Ludlow SY8 1DR
01584-876000

Some two years after moving out of Riddings Park (see p72), Ludlow Town finally moved into their plush new surroundings in July 2003. The £1.8m Coors Stadium in the shadow of the A49 trunk road on the northern side of the town had been under construction for the previous year and was opened with a County Cup match against Shrewsbury Town which pulled in 2,000 curious fans.

The slip road to the A49 provides a great vantage point to survey the venue and the attractive backdrop of Whitcliffe Wood. Straddling the first and second team pitches is the stylish pavilion building, very much the centre of the development. Upstairs is a range of bars and lounges, with viewing balconies facing onto both pitches. Downstairs are the changing facilities and offices. Both pitches are railed, floodlit and benefit from seating placed beneath the balcony overhang of the pavilion. The rest of the accommodation is flat standing, although plans exist for a 600-seater stand on the A49 side of the ground if Ludlow's League status demands it.

There are two further pitches on the complex for the use of Ludlow's junior sides, making four in total. The five-year naming rights deal with Burton-based brewer Coors is a major coup for Ludlow, especially since the only other venue bearing Coors' name is Coors Field, the Major League baseball park in Denver, USA. In that sense, Ludlow are in exalted company, but it remains to be seen if they can be just as upwardly mobile on the field as they are off it.

Market Drayton Town F.C.

Greenfields Sports Club,
Greenfields Lane, Market Drayton TF9 3SL
01630-655088

A new name for an old club – a sure sign of ambition. By changing from Little Drayton Rangers to Market Drayton Town, the club was also signifying that it should be the town's true representatives in the football pyramid. Quite what Drayton Town – the Shropshire County League side that uses the other pitch at Greenfields – thought of the move is not recorded.

Market Drayton themselves only left the County League in 1998, climbing into the Premier Division of the West Midlands League after just one season, but the ground has kept pace with the team.

Set in the Little Drayton area of the town, Greenfields is a large sporting area with the town's rugby club on one side of the lane and the Sports Club on the other. Market Drayton use the railed-off pitch in the far corner of the complex, so they have built separate changing and hospitality facilities. There is an impressive set of corner-mounted floodlights and a traditional-looking stand along the west touchline. The depth of this stand lends it a box-like appearance, but the view is helped by an upwards-sloping roof, and the green cladding can make it seem camouflaged. If Market Drayton were to move up a level to the Midland Alliance, they would have to destroy the rural, accessible feel to this attractive ground by hiding it behind some hideous tin fence. At this point, success becomes a double-edged sword.

Milton United F.C.
Leek Road, Milton,
Stoke-on-Trent ST2 7AF

Thankfully the small Potteries village of Milton still has a football club, so their hidden gem of a football ground will stay in use. Having changed name to Milton Rangers in 2001, the club resigned from the Springbank Vending Midland League in 2003 but resurfaced in the Staffordshire County League after taking the place of their reserve team and reverting to the old name. Despite being on the main A5009 road, the ground truly is hidden with an entrance concealed between the primary school and the community centre leading to a tiny car park. The pitch has been set into a hill and levelled as much as possible, so that it sits above the entrance but seems to be holding back the large bank behind the top goal.

A splendid view of the ground and the village can be had from the heights of Carmountside Cemetery just to the south. The sections of cover on the north side, essentially 'lean-to' designs attached to the school's Victorian brickwork, can clearly be

seen. A further basic cover used to stand on the south side of the pitch until the mid-1990s. If you like tight, enclosed grounds in characterful urban settings, Milton United is your nirvana.

Top: The north side in 2003
Centre: The cover that formerly stood on the south side, seen in 1994 (pic: Bob Lilliman)
Bottom: The view from the cemetery in 2003.

Newcastle Town F.C.

Lyme Valley Parkway Stadium,
Lilleshall Road,
Newcastle-under-Lyme ST5 3BX
01782-662351

Aerial views taken just after the opening of the Lyme Valley Parkway Stadium (LVPS) show a very basic sportsground in a somewhat barren and treeless setting. As the LVPS nears its Jubilee, however, the area has matured into a very pleasant parkland, with the well developed stadium nestling peacefully in the landscaped valley.

The velodrome that surrounds the pitch may add to the viewing distances, but the flowing lines of the cycling track make a fairly ordinary stadium much more interesting.

From the main entrance, most of the facilities are to your left, on the east side of the stadium. The pavilion building, the only structure dating back to the opening of the venue, sits below the track and has had its view blocked by the addition of a small stand for officials. Just beyond this is the deep stand, containing ten rows of seats

*Above:& Below: The grandstand and covered terrace at various points in the 1990s (pics: Andy Dakin) **Bottom**: A panoramic view in 2002.*

under a boxy roof. Opposite is a narrow terrace, covered by a solid roof and festooned with advertising hoardings.

The LVPS has a Unibond League grading and although it might take a reorganisation in non-League football for Newcastle to get there, the ground won't look out of place.

Norton United F.C.

Norton CC & MW Institute,
Community Drive, Smallthorne,
Stoke ST6 1RU
01782-838290

Norton Colliery closed down in 1977 but the spacious welfare ground has remained strong as Norton United have risen out of relative obscurity into the North-West Counties League.

A hilly approach to Community Drive is almost inevitable, and you wonder how there can be enough flat land for a football ground, let alone a cricket field. The Institute has been laid out on two levels, with the cricket pitch and clubhouse set above the football ground, which is reached by a path skirting the far side of the club from the car park.

The path comes out at the top of a grass bank alongside the halfway line. In the far left corner, a cage-like tunnel has been built for the players. To the left of the halfway line, at the foot of the bank, there is a thirty-yard stretch of cover, half given to standing and half containing red plastic seats which have a restricted view if anyone is using the standing space.

The other three sides are open flat standing, with dugouts set on the tree-lined north side of the pitch. The ground's best feature lies beyond the far goal – a splendid view out over the Ford Green valley to the settlement of Norton-in-the-Moors.

The ground is shared by Norton AG of the Springbank Vending Midland League, who formed in 2002 as a result of a merger between Adderley Green and Leoni AG.

R.A.F. Cosford Stadium

R.A.F. Cosford Airbase,
Albrighton,
Wolverhampton WV7 3EX
01902-372393

Incredible as it now seems, a hangar at RAF Cosford was the home of British indoor athletics for over two decades until the National Indoor Arena opened in Birmingham. The indoor track at Cosford has since been demolished, but the pleasant outdoor stadium survives.

Now used by the youth teams of Wolverhampton Wanderers as well as servicemen, Cosford has a modern synthetic running track and all the usual athletics paraphernalia. There is also an elevated stand on the west side of the track which dates from the 1960s and looks like a scaled down version of the stand at Croydon Arena.

One unusual feature, for a non-League ground at least, is an electronic scoreboard on the east side of the stadium. A modern pavilion building at the south end provides good quality facilities for the track and surrounding sports fields.

Obviously, no team from the base competes in a public league, and it is faintly ironic that the only time RAF Cosford have competed in such a league was in wartime. A team from the base played in the wartime Birmingham League.

Cosford base is also home to a major part of the Royal Air Force Museum collection.

Rocester F.C.

The Hillsfield, Mill Street, Rocester,
Uttoxeter ST14 5JX
01889-590463

Hillsfield is a fastidiously neat and tidy ground set at the back of the small village of Rocester, which is internationally famous as the home of JCB excavators. It was only opened in 1987 but has been steadily added to and was deemed good enough to allow Rocester to take their place in the Southern League in 1999.

From Mill Street, a track snakes round the pitch to the car park on the north side. Here is a modern single-storey pitched-roof clubhouse with a narrow overhang cover facing onto the pitch. Next to this is a modest, almost polite grandstand with 200 green seats under another pitched roof. In the centre of the opposite side is a small area of covered standing, and a few yards behind the east goal is the county border with Derbyshire.

The ground would be completely unremarkable were it not for the looming (no pun intended) presence of an abandoned cotton mill at the village end of the ground. There was already a corn mill on the site, watered by the River Dove, and this was bought by the son of the revolutionary cotton-spinner Sir Richard Arkwright. Arkwright junior, also called Richard, converted the mill for cotton production and expanded hugely but the mill fell out of use some time ago.

Hillsfield is shared by Ashbourne United, who seem to prefer Hillsfield to the scenic Recreation Ground in Ashbourne itself, which has a cover but no cotton mill.

Shifnal Town F.C.

Phoenix Park, Coppice Green Lane,
Shifnal TF11 8PB
01952-463667

Marking the eastern boundary of developed Shifnal, Phoenix Park is a tidy and impressive ground which offers no hint of the club's chequered history over the last 25 years. In 1982, Shifnal Town had just won a second successive West Midlands League title, but as a number of rival clubs migrated to the expanding Southern League, floodlight-less Shifnal had to stay put and four years later were nearly out of existence when housing was built on their Admiral's Park ground (see p78).

Town managed to develop a field next to Idsall Sports Centre into a new ground, appropriately named Phoenix Park. In reducing the slope of the field, substantial earth banks were created around the north-east corner of the ground. An excellent elevated cantilever stand was built on the western touchline and, most crucially, Phoenix Park was equipped with flood- lights which enabled Town to become founder members of the Midland Alliance in 1994.

Unfortunately, Shifnal struggled to be effective at the new level and suffered relegation in 2003, but few would bet against them coming back even stronger. Shifnal Town thrives in adversity.

Stapenhill F.C.

Edgehill, Maple Grove, Stapenhill,
Burton-on-Trent DE15 9NN
01283-562471

The more pedantic reader will point out that Stapenhill's ground is actually in Derbyshire, but since the drive that leads to it is in Staffordshire, I think we can justify its inclusion. A further geographic curiosity is that Stapenhill are currently regrouping in the Leicestershire Senior League after a disastrous 2001/02 season that saw the club leave the Midland Alliance without seeing out the season. It was a sad way to leave for a club which, like Shifnal, was a founder member, but Stapenhill are going well in their new League and could be back in the Alliance soon.

Edgehill is at the back of a 1950s council housing estate and is protected by a concrete panel fence. The social club stands just outside the ground, next to a large car park.

Above: The bizarre press stand before a section of cover was added to the right
Bottom: The cover with a seated centre section, and the backdrop of Drakelow Power Station (pics: Andy Dakin).

Along the western touchline is a long, low cover with seats in the centre section. The most bizarre feature of the ground is to the right of the entrance, where a two-tier structure rises behind the goal. Ostensibly for the use of the press, it is difficult to fathom why the stand was built and it must be a diverting target for wayward strikers. Between this structure and the entrance is a further section of cover.

Stone Dominoes F.C.

Springbank Stadium,
Hilderstone Road, Meir Heath,
Stoke-on-Trent ST3 7NY
01782-388465

***Below**: The rather less developed ground when Meir KA were the main occupants (pic Andy Dakin)*

The only club in this book with a lease on two grounds, Stone Dominoes has a history which is as remarkable as it is brief. Formed as a boys' team in 1987, Dominoes – named as a corruption of St Dominic's Church Scout Group from which the original team was formed – entered open-age football in 1995 and three subsequent promotions have taken them to Division One of the North-West Counties League.

Springbank Stadium (named after the Doms' principal sponsor) was originally home to Midland Combination outfit Meir KA (Kings Arms), and had been known variously as Hilderstone Road, Stanley Park and Kings Park. Unable to gain permission for floodlights at their ground in Yarnfield (see p47), Dominoes took over the lease at Hilderstone Road, with Meir becoming ground-sharers. Stone spent a reported £60,000 upgrading the ground and moved in during the 2001/02 season.

A concrete fence encloses the ground, which stands on the edge of the countryside to the south of Stoke. Backing onto the car park is a stand running the width of the pitch behind the goal. This has 250 seats but the roof is below the height of the crossbar, so you can judge the quality of the view for yourself. The pavilion in the corner is just about the only recognisable surviving part of the old Meir ground, which used to also stage cricket. On the west side of the pitch is another low cover, this time for standing, so one wonders if there is a height restriction imposed by the planning authorities. Dominoes clearly intend to keep toppling the opposition on their way up the Pyramid, but is this ground going to find favour with neutrals? I doubt it.

Wem Town

Butler Sports Centre,
Bowens Field, Wem
SY4 5AP
01939-233287

We have listed this ground under Wem Town, who ply their trade in the Shropshire County League, but the venue also stages the home games of the more senior Shawbury United of the West Midlands League.

Wem is a small market town on the River Roden and is old enough to have been mentioned in the Doomsday Book. More recently, the Butler Sports Centre was opened in 1975 by the former Wolves and England captain Billy Wright, easily the most famous footballer produced by Shropshire.

Just off the town centre, the centrepiece of the complex is the floodlit football pitch, which is neatly railed off and has hard standing all round. In front of the clubhouse is a plain, flat-roofed stand with blue seats either side of the players tunnel. The dugouts are on the opposite side of the field and these have doors for protection when the ground is not in use.

Like Market Drayton, much of the charm

of the ground derives from the open and accessible feel of the place. In the words of Cole Porter, sung by Bing Crosby in 1944, "Give me land, lots of land under starry skies above, Don't fence me in."

Whitchurch Alport F.C.

Yockings Park, Black Park Road,
Whitchurch SY13 1PG
01948-667415

Below: *Yockings Park's splendidly restored grandstand looking rather healthier than in the second picture (by Andy Dakin) from around 1990*

Shropshire's only representative in the Mid-Cheshire League is one of non-League's steadier outfits, having been continuous members since the MCL was founded in 1948. Players of that era would still recognise the ground today as it hasn't changed a great deal since it opened on 29th August 1923 when the old Cheshire League Whitchurch club thrashed Chester 4-1. Soon after there was a game against Crewe that attracted a crowd of 3,500 at a time when the population of the town was only 5,700.

When Yockings Park opened, contemporary reports described the grandstand as "new and commodious" and for an octogenarian structure the stand is in rude health. As part of a sympathetic restoration in recent years, the walls have been painted white and the roof given a fetching russet coat.

Between the stand and the entrance is the clubhouse and the rest of the ground has flat standing. Old maps of the ground show a cover behind the south goal which was probably there at the opening but seems to have disappeared in the 1960s.

The current club formed in 1946 and added Alport after Alport Farm, which was the home of a local footballer killed in World War Two.

Wolverhampton Casuals F.C.

Brinsford Lane, Coven Heath,
Wolverhampton WV10 7PR
01902-783214

If Bing Crosby was singing "Don't Fence Me In" about Wem Town, then fellow crooner Perry Como may have dedicated "There's No Place Like Home (For the Holidays)" to the Brinsford Lane ground of Wolverhampton Casuals. The club was forced to spend a number of seasons playing in the large but soulless Aldersley Stadium in Wolverhampton whilst a long campaign to add floodlights to this rural ground was fought. This eventually happened in 1998 and Casuals were able to play their West Midlands League Premier Division games back in Coven Heath.

Brinsford Lane is just off the A449 to the north of Wolverhampton, a few hundred yards into Staffordshire, and this attractive ground is naturally enclosed by bushes and trees. The driveway runs behind the goal to a parking area next to the clubhouse. The only cover is a plain but solid stand erected in the early 1990s containing bench seating. Obviously, this is not one of the more developed grounds in the region but what it lacks in sophistication is more than made up in charm.

Further down Brinsford Lane is Featherstone Prison, now fielding a team in the Staffordshire County League.

Audley & District F.C.

Town Fields, Old Road, Bignall End, Stoke-on-Trent ST7 8QH
01782-544232

Bignall End is an area founded on coal-mining, so it's difficult to tell which of the many hills in the area are legacies of the 'black gold'. One such hill towers over the trim Town Fields ground of Audley, now in their 16th Springbank Vending Midland League season.

The hill, which even has picnic tables provided towards the summit, gives a splendid view over the ground and Bignall End itself. Town Fields has no cover yet but the facilities are modern, including two pitches and an all-weather training area.

Ball Haye Green F.C.

Ball Haye Green WMC, Ball Haye Green, Leek ST13 6BH
01538-371926

Thought to have been used since around 1918, this is one of the more interesting grounds in the Midland League, tucked away behind the Working Mens Club in the claustrophobic Ball Haye Green suburb of Leek.

The sheer face of a massive industrial building encloses one side of the field, dwarfing a stretch of standing cover running from the halfway line to an old-style pavilion in the corner of the pitch.

There is flat hard-standing all round and the ground has been floodlit for over ten years. As founder (and surviving) members of the Midland League, it's hard to believe that Ball Haye Green are only the third most senior club in Leek after Leek Town and Leek CSOB.

Brereton Social F.C.

Red Lion Ground, Armitage Lane, Brereton, Rugeley WS15 1EB

01889-585526

Brereton have fallen on hard times since leaving the top division of the West Midlands League in 1987, but they are still the nearest thing to a town team for Rugeley.

The ground, which takes its name from the public house just the other side of the A51, has also suffered in recent seasons with the demolition of the grandstand. This was rather a basic structure set back from the pitch but the ground feels incomplete without it.

The floodlights have stood since the 1970s and were upgraded in 1995 when Social acquired the bulbs from Hednesford Town's former home at Cross Keys.

The cooling towers of Rugeley Power Station make for an imposing backdrop.

Above: The stand and pavilion in 1983 (by Bob Lilliman)
Below: The stand in 1997 showing the unusual layout set back from the pitch.

Burntwood Town F.C.

Memorial Ground, Rugeley Road, Burntwood WS7 9BE

07931-626887

Visiting this intimate ground in Autumn, there are so many leaves on the field it's difficult to tell where the pitch ends and the trees begin. The pitch has been cut into a bank, so it's set well above the entrance and the large memorial hall in the centre of Burntwood.

On the far side of the ground is a basic but useful cover made of scaffold poles and some corrugated iron sheeting.

Eccleshall F.C.

Pershall Park, Chester Road, Pershall, Staffordshire ST21 6NE
01785-851351

As the name suggests, this rural ground is just off the main road in the tiny village of Pershall, to the west of charming Eccleshall. During 2003 the ground was enclosed by a wooden fence to enable Eccleshall's step up to the North-West Counties League. The next step for this ambitious club will be to install floodlights, and perhaps build a new grandstand.

At present there are two covers, one sandwiched between the dugouts and the other formed by an overhang to the pavilion, which is set in the corner directly by the entrance. Our pictures show the far side cover before and after the ground enclosure and a spot of repainting.

Florence F.C.

Florence Miners Welfare, Lightwood Road, Stoke-on-Trent ST3 4JS
01782-312887

Few grounds can have experienced a change in setting as dramatic as Florence in the last decade. The three pitheads of Florence Colliery – named after one of the Duke of Sutherland's daughters – used to tower above the west end of the ground but following closure in the 1990s the Colliery was flattened to make way for housing.

Florence have greatly improved the ground since then, adding a small cover to the south side of the pitch and gradually tidying up the fringes of the site. The car park and clubhouse sit above the pitch, enabling a fine view of the ground and the landscaped spoil heaps left behind by 116 years of mining at Florence.

Foley F.C.

Whitcombe Road, Meir, Stoke-on-Trent ST3 6AU
01782-595274

The approach to Foley FC is unpromising – a pot-holed private road off the A520 in Meir – making the revelation of the hidden ground all the more pleasant a surprise. Set in a hollow, you enter at the top of a bank in the south-east corner. To the right is a grass bank behind the goal with crush barriers laid out here and there. Immediately to the left, next to the pitch, is a cover with a sloping roof and a few chairs underneath. By the time you read this, Foley's friendly band of volunteers may have erected the home-made floodlight pylons they've been working on.

Goldenhill Wanderers F.C.

Sandyford Cricket Club, Shelford Road, Stoke-on-Trent ST6 5LA

Goldenhill's pitch occupies part of a large sports ground on the northern edge of the Potteries. The pavilion is next to the entrance, leaving a fair walk to the railed-off pitch. Between the dugouts is a tiny cover which tends to be used as much by substitutes and trainers as spectators. The other notable feature of the ground is the overhead power line running across the pitch.

There is usually a club sharing Shelford Road with Goldenhill, and in 2003/04 County League rookies Manor Inne have replaced Vale Juniors (who became Vale Victoria and moved to Biddulph) in this capacity.

Great Wyrley F.C.

Hazelbrook, Hazel Lane, Great Wyrley, Cannock WS6 6AA
01922-410366

As this book went to press, earthmovers were in action at Hazelbrook, making trenches for floodlight cabling as part of an upgrade that may also see a stand built on the far side of the ground.

Great Wyrley's ground – shared by Sikh Hunters FC – is opposite the entrance to the demolished Harrisons ground (see p67) in Hazel Lane, just off the A34. A small metal cover right by the entrance is the only shelter at present, but there is plenty of space in the massive 'Hazelbrook Suite' building which completely dominates the ground, making this as much a social centre as a sporting one.

Hanley Town F.C.

Abbey Lane, Abbey Hulton, Stoke-on-Trent ST2 8AJ
01782-267234

Hulton Abbey was founded in 1219 and was closed down by Henry VIII, but many of the place and street names in the area derive from the Cistercian abbey. Off one such street is the exposed ground of Hanley Town, now in the Midland League after prolonged spells in the Mid-Cheshire League. Once through the driveway into the ground, the clubhouse is in the south-east corner to your left, with a small overhang for shelter.

On the far side of the ground is a small, basic, blue-and-white-painted cover bearing the club name on the back wall. Beyond this is a distant view over the densely packed housing of Birches Head. Hanley have a difficult job to lure fans away from their many local rivals, not to mention the area's Football League duo, but the ground has plenty of potential to develop.

Mile Oak Rovers & Youth F.C.
Price Avenue, Mile Oak, Tamworth B78 3NL
01827-289614

Mile Oak's firm roots in the community of this quiet suburb of Tamworth have kept the club going through some difficult times since Rovers left the Midland Combination in 1994. 2003 saw Rovers make a second attempt to start back up the pyramid by rejoining the Combination's lowest division.

Mile Oak first played at Price Avenue in 1967 after playing on numerous grounds around Tamworth including the Castle Pleasure Grounds, a former home of Tamworth Castle FC. A clubhouse was built in 1971 (much extended since), and the small stand appeared four years later. The addition of floodlights in 1984 was the final piece in a jigsaw that saw Mile Oak assume the mantle of senior club in Tamworth for a number of seasons due to The Lambs' sojourn in the West Midlands League. In 1985 Price Avenue became one of the least developed grounds of recent years to have hosted Southern League football but Mile Oak lasted for only four seasons. The ground today is virtually unchanged from those glory years.

Morda United F.C.
Weston Road, Morda, Oswestry SY10 9NS
01691-659621

Most neutrals are pleasantly surprised with what they find at Morda's pretty village ground on Weston Road. A paybox guards the entrance, from where a road runs behind the goal to a small parking area. The pitch is sunk below this road, making it a great place to watch from.

On the north side of the pitch is a superb 120-seat grandstand, a modern construction built in a traditional style and finished in dark green cladding. Given the basic nature of some of the grounds in the lower divisions of the West Midlands League, Morda is a gem that we can be proud to have in English football.

National Sports Centre, Lilleshall

Pave Lane, Lilleshall, Near Newport, Shropshire TF10 9AT
01952-603003

One of Sport England's major centres of activity, Lilleshall is featured here because of the unique semi-circular cover which adorns the artificial pitch in the middle of this vast complex (picture by Mick Blakeman).

Of course, Lilleshall has a considerable footballing pedigree, having been home to the FA's National School of Excellence from 1984 to 1999 and a key training venue for England's victorious 1966 World Cup squad. It is also quite normal to see top players taking advantage of Lilleshall's renowned rehabilitation facilities, or professional clubs using one of the many top class grass pitches. Lilleshall Hall, the heart of the complex, was built in 1829 and its purchase by the Central Council of Physical Recreation in 1949 was "made possible by a financial gift from the people of South Africa" according to Lilleshall's own literature. The Centre was opened in 1951 by the then Princess Elizabeth in a ceremony presided over by Sir Stanley Rous.

Rowley Park Stadium

Averill Road, Stafford ST17 9SX
01785-251060

In 2003/04 Rowley Park is without a regular tenant in a recognised pyramid league, but the venue is noteworthy as a former home of Stafford Town (formerly known as Rising Brook and now tenants of Stafford Rangers) and Brocton (who moved to the much larger Cannock Stadium in 2002).

Rowley Park is a municipal athletics venue with a continental feel to it. Cut into a bank on the west side of the track is a small section of uncovered bench seating, behind which is a facilities block with a covered viewing area at the front.

Stone Dominoes F.C. (Headquarters)
Springbank Park, Yarnfield Road, Yarnfield, Stone ST15 0NF
01782-761891

Opened in 1995, the lack of floodlights at Yarnfield has forced Dominoes' first team to play home games at Meir Heath (see page 36), but this is still a thoroughly impressive set-up. An award-winning groundstaff maintains four immaculate railed-off pitches although none of these have cover.

Amongst the teams playing here are Dominoes' second string and Stone Old Alleynians, both in the Staffs County League. Port Vale's academy is also based here, as are Stone Dominoes Ladies.

Just in front of the pavilion building is a unique monument dedicated to the club – four outsized black dominoes ranged in an arc. Holes cut in the dominoes create the numbers 1-9-8-7, the year of Stone's formation, and a plaque states "Stone Dominoes FC – Founded on Truth". The dominoes are eerily reminiscent of the mysterious monolith seen in the opening sequence of the film '2001: A Space Odyssey'. Personally, I wonder if Stone Dominoes is more of a movement than a football club.

Telford Athletics Stadium
New Road, Oakengates, Telford TF2 7AB
01952-612680

No New Town is complete without its municipal athletics stadium, and Telford have one of the exposed, windswept and underused variety. The infield is used for football, we understand by White Horse Rangers of the Telford Combination, and the presence of a covered stand on the south side of the pitch merits the inclusion of the stadium in this book.

The stand has clearly seen better days as it would appear that the seating decks have been removed at some point. The remaining seats appear to have been provided for various timing and drug-testing officials.

Wrockwardine Wood F.C.
New Road, Oakengates, Telford TF2 7AB
01952-613086

The New Road ground, next-door to Telford Athletics Stadium, is now used by the Shropshire County League Wrockwardine Wood which was formerly suffixed by 'United'. On the eve of the 2003/04 season the Wrockwardine Wood side competing in the West Midlands League withdrew due to a shortage of players. This was despite the club having made some modest improvements such as the new post and rail barrier. The small cover on the south side of the pitch is thought to date from Wood's earlier spell in the West Midlands League, which lasted from 1965 to 1970.

Yates Club Ground
Lime Lane, Pelsall, Staffordshire WS3 5AS

This is a real obscurity, a ground which defies any categorisation beyond that of 'non-League' in the widest sense. The Yates empire was founded on moving freight by barge – a kind of Eddie Stobart of the canal network. The ground in Lime Lane was opened in 1967 for the use of the works team and appropriately borders the Cannock Essington Canal. The social club was built in 1973.

After the decline of the Yates team the owner decided to take a speculative approach to the ground and in 1993 laid the base of a concrete and breezeblock stand on the canal bank. This was never quite finished and no team in the pyramid has been lured here, possibly because the pitch is too narrow.

The last few years have seen a number of improvements to this odd little ground. The two sides bordering the caravan park have received a smart green fence, and a post and rail barrier has appeared on the canal side, complete with advertising hoardings. Since the pictures were taken, a rather makeshift cover has appeared (see page 92) in front of the concrete steps, but it doesn't look particularly storm-proof. The best chance to see a game here is Sunday morning.

Other Grounds

The remaining grounds staging football at County League level are summarised here, by County and then by League. The key to the Leagues is: SVML – Springbank Vending Midland League; WML – West Midlands League; MC – Midland Combination; STCL – Staffordshire County League; SHCL – Shropshire County League.

STAFFORDSHIRE

ABBEY HULTON UNITED (SVML)
Birches Head Road, Abbey Hulton, Stoke ST2 8DD
Neatly railed pitch at the foot of a steep hill, lacking cover at present but plenty of scenery to look at.

ALSAGERS BANK (STCL)
The Drive, Alsagers Bank, Newcastle ST7 8BB
Basic facilities, unrailed pitch set in a small village between Newcastle and the M6.

BILBROOK (WML)
Pendeford Lane, Wolverhampton WV9 5HQ
New entrants in 2003, Bilbrook have taken over the former Wombourne Hockey Club ground, built in 1965. This has two pitches separated by the clubhouse, one with training lights and one used by the first team with new dugouts.

BROCTON RESERVES (STCL)
Chetwynd Arms Ground, Cannock Road, Brocton ST17 0ST
Brocton FC was formed in 1937 when the then owner of the Chetwynd Arms pub donated a football to local youngsters and told them to start a team. 66 years later, the pitch next to the pub is still lovingly maintained and is the home to the reserve team after the enforced departure of the first team to more advanced grounds. The pitch is roped off for games, and there are training lights.

CHEADLE TOWN OB (SVML)
South Moorlands Leisure Centre, Allen Road, Cheadle ST10 1HJ
Railed-off pitch next to a modern leisure centre just off the town centre. No cover.

ENVILLE ATHLETIC (MC)
Hall Drive, Enville, Nr Stourbridge DY7 5HB
South-West Staffordshire is no football hotbed and some decent-sized towns such as Kinver and Wombourne have no significant grounds. The team from the tiny village of Enville plays in the grounds of the imposing Enville Hall, on a pitch shared by cricket. An unusual setting but the ground has no cover.

FEATHERSTONE PRISON (STCL)
HMP Featherstone, New Road, Wolverhampton WV10 7PU
Featherstone made a return to 'public' football in 2003 some six years after an experimental season in the old Division Two of the Midland League and we believe them to be the only prison team in a pyramid league. All their matches are played at home where the main football pitch has dugouts and a small amount of cover created by a wooden overhang to a disused toilet block by a corner of the pitch. There are strict restrictions on photography at this ground.

FOUR ASHES GROUND
Station Drive, Four Ashes, Staffs WV10 7BU
Like the Yates Club ground, Four Ashes is another oddity without a fixed tenant club. The ground belongs to the Four Ashes Inn, and until the Summer of 2003 had a metal cover (pictured) at the side of the pitch, although there was no post & rail barrier. The owner of the ground then decided to completely re-seed the field and demolished the cover, replacing it with a temporary 'back-of-a-lorry' stand of the type seen at West Midlands Police's Tally Ho ground. It remains to be seen if the ground will ever stage football in the pyramid.

HOLDITCH MINERS WELFARE (STCL)
London Road, Chesterton, Newcastle ST5 7PT
In Roman times, Holditch was the first recorded place in North Staffordshire where mining took place, and although the modern colliery closed in 1989, the modernised Welfare club is going strong. This is a partially railed pitch on the main road between Newcastle and Chesterton.

Right: FOUR ASHES F.C.

Other Grounds

HOLT JCB (STCL)
JCB Lakeside Club, B5030, Rocester, Uttoxeter ST14 5LS
Well-maintained pitch in the grounds of the internationally famous JCB World HQ, which is built around two man-made lakes. Holt JCB is actually the name of part of the dealer network attached to the company.

PENKRIDGE TOWN (STCL)
Rodbaston Agricultural College, Rodbaston Drive, Penkridge ST19 5PQ
Penkridge formerly played on a ground in the town but in 2002 moved south to a pitch in the grounds of Rodbaston College. This has no cover or pitch enclosure, but Penkridge have plans to create a new floodlit ground at the College on a field previously used for turnip cultivation.

REDGATE CLAYTON (SVML)
Northwood Lane, Clayton, Newcastle ST5 4BN
Former home of Parkway Clayton before they joined forces with Newcastle Town, the successful town club playing at LymeValley Parkway Stadium. The railed-off ground has no cover although you might be able to get shelter by the clubhouse and still be able to see the game.

RIVERWAY (WML)
Stafford Cricket & Hockey Club, Riverway, Stafford ST16 3TH
Basic facilities contained within a large sports ground in Stafford town centre, flanked by the River Sow.

SHENSTONE PATHFINDER (WML)
Shenstone Pavilion Club, Birmingham Road, Shenstone, Lichfield WS14 0JR
Partially railed pitch behind the homely Bulls Head pub on the main road in Shenstone. No cover but a smart pair of perspex dugouts.

STALLINGTON (SVML)
Fulford Lane, off Stallington Road, Blythe Bridge, Stoke ST11 9QJ
The very epitome of a rural ground, accessed via a gate down a narrow country road. The railed-off pitch occupies a clearing in the woods, with a tiny amount of cover formed by the overhang of the 1960s clubhouse set behind the north goal (*photo right*).

WEDGWOOD (STCL)
Wedgwood Sports & Social Club, Wedgwood Drive, Barlaston, Stoke ST12 9ER
The sensitively landscaped Wedgwood works at Barlaston was built between 1938 and 1940, and a sports ground laid out to the south of Wedgwood Drive. The pitch is railed but has no cover, and is overlooked by the imposing Barlaston Hall, which was built in 1756. Few grounds in Britain have such a grand approach as that past the hall into the Wedgwood complex (*photo below*).

WEST CANNOCK COLLIERY SPORTS GROUND
Bradbury Road, Pye Green, Cannock WS12 4EP
The former home of Cannock Chase FC (known originally as Hednesford Progressive) is now used by local league sides Keys FC and Winding Wheel FC, as well as Hednesford Town Youth. The railed pitch has a small brick shelter on the south side which is a blessing on such an exposed ground, as is the large social club.

WOLSTANTON UNITED (SVML)
Bradwell Community Centre, Riceyman Road, Bradwell, Stoke ST5 8LF
Railed-off but cover-less pitch at the side of a community centre in the middle of a housing estate.

Other Grounds

WYRLEY RANGERS (WML)
Long Lane Park, Long Lane, Essington, Staffs WV11 2AA
A section of cover is just about the only thing missing at this impressive new ground set in open countryside. A large clubhouse looks out onto a fully railed and floodlit pitch which is surrounded by high mesh fencing. Wyrley recently absorbed the rival Marston Wolves team and this is a club to keep an eye on.

Above : Wyrley Rangers

SHROPSHIRE

BELVIDERE COLTS (SHCL)
Sundorne Pitches, Sundorne Road, Shrewsbury SY1 4RQ
Sundorne is probably the largest municipal sports ground in Shrewsbury and although various County League teams have used pitches here, none of them have any spectator facilities.

BISHOP'S CASTLE (Montgomeryshire League)
Brampton Road Playing Fields, Bishop's Castle SY9 5BB
A South Shropshire side more comfortable in Welsh football, Bishop's Castle playing fields has a well maintained pitch with a post and rail barrier running down one side but no cover. It's located on the main A488 at the town's main crossroads.

BROSELEY JUNIORS (SHCL)
Birchmeadow, Cockshot Lane, Broseley, Telford TF12 5LL
A council type recreation ground with the main football pitch near to the entrance. This has a post and rail surround painted white and a plain brick building in the corner by the entrance for changing. Birchmeadow has portable dugouts and a grass bank handy for viewing. Also used by Broseley Colts and Broseley Athletic in recent years.

BROWN CLEE (SHCL)
Hall Meadow, Cleobury North WV16 6RS
This is a large field behind the village shop and part of it is marked out as the pitch but only by walking half-way across it until you find the touchline can you tell that it is sometimes used for football. The goalposts are kept in a shed at the back of the village shop and put up and taken down for every game.

CHURCH STRETTON TOWN (SHCL)
Russell's Meadow, Essex Road, Church Stretton SY6 6AX
Four pitches as part of a general facility for the town. There is a small pavilion with a veranda but nothing else. It is first proper turn on the right as you come into the town over the railway and then straight in front of you.

CLEE HILL UNITED (SHCL)
Knowle Sports Ground, Tenbury Road, Knowle SY8 3NE
This is actually in the village of Knowle near Clee Hill and is a small sports field in the village. There are changing rooms and a small car park. It was left by a (presumably dead) resident and bought as an amenity for the village in 1974. Used for cricket in the summer and they also hold second hand sales there every week to help with the village sports club fund.

CRAVEN ARMS TOWN (SHCL)
Craven Arms Playing Fields, Shrewsbury Road, Craven Arms SY7 8BX
Two pitches next to the community centre which has rooms for things like exercise classes and changing rooms. There is also a covered walkway outside and the building looks much more like a sports building than some other Shropshire village grounds. You could watch in some comfort from the walkway.

DRAYTON TOWN (SHCL)
Greenfields Sports Ground, Greenfields Lane, Market Drayton TF9 3SL
Unrailed pitch at the entrance to the sports ground also used by Market Drayton Town (see page 28).

Other Grounds

ELLESMERE RANGERS (SHCL)
Beech Grove, Ellesmere SY12 0BS
Currently successful on the pitch, Ellesmere's ground is set in the middle of a post-war housing estate and has a fully railed pitch, dugouts and a pavilion but no cover.

HANWOOD UNITED (SHCL)
Main Road, Hanwood, Shrewsbury SY5 8LY
On the right just past the railway bridge as you leave the village coming from Shrewsbury. The ground has a typically attractive Shropshire setting with hills to the north, and is barriered with post and wire. The dugouts are splendidly tatty (note how much larger the home one is) and the ground has a certain potential.

HAUGHMOND (SHCL)
Mereside, Springfield, Shrewsbury SY2 6LF
Following the departure of Belle Vue OB from the County League in 2003, Haughmond moved across town from the Sundorne pitches to occupy this community ground close to the A5. The ground has a tubular metal barrier but no cover, and has a very open feel.

HIGHLEY WELFARE (SHCL)
Main Road, Highley WV16 6NG
The Miners Welfare Club and Recreation Ground occupy a large area in the middle of this large but isolated village to the south of Bridgnorth. Surprisingly, the ground has no spectator facilities or even a pitch surround despite having staged football since the 1920s.

HOPESGATE UNITED (SHCL)
The Coates, Snailbeach SY5 0LZ
Picturesque ground which is literally 'off the beaten track' in an obscure village founded on a lead mine which ceased production in 1955. The Coates was used by recent County League side Snailbeach White Star, and is now home to Hopesgate. A discreet and fading sign points the way to the ground down a winding track that opens out into a field large enough for two pitches, each with dugouts of differing styles but no permanent railing. The stunning scenery here gives the ground an alpine feel, much like Newcastle.

MEOLE BRACE (SHCL)
Church Road, Meole Brace, Shrewsbury SY3 9HQ
A dilapidated post and rail, a decent car park and a changing room cum community centre block that is less dilapidated than the post and rail but not as tidy as the car park. Meole Brace has a feel of an entirely separate village yet it is right in Shrewsbury's built up area.

NEWCASTLE (Mid-Wales South League)
The Mill Field, Newcastle-on-Clun SY7 8QN
One of the great unsung outposts of English football, and I bet you've never heard of this place. Newcastle is a few miles west of Clun, where Shropshire bulges into Wales. The ground is to the south of the main B4368, but you have to walk across other fields to reach it. There is a welcoming sign at the entrance, but facilities are pretty basic, with just a small shelter on the south side of the pitch behind a stake-and-wire barrier. The Mill Field's selling point is the stunning scenery provided by the dense Clun Forest and the ridge of Spoad Hill as seen in the photo above.

Below: Hopesgate United

Other Grounds

NEWPORT TOWN (WML)
Shuker's Field, Barnmeadow Road, Newport TF10 7SG
In order to gain promotion to the Premier Division of the WML, Newport's first team has had to leave the unlit Shuker's Field ground to share at Wolverhampton Casuals (see page 39). The ground is announced by a huge sign on the side of the modern changing block and although it is railed with dugouts, there is no cover here.

OAKENGATES TOWN (SHCL)
School Grove, Oakengates, Telford TF2 6BQ
Oakengates came close to abandoning this ground in 2003 but have stayed put. The ground has a few tired sections of post and rail barrier, and a fortified wooden changing block with an overhang next to the pitch.

Below: Oakengates Town (pic: Mick Blakeman)

OSWESTRY BOYS CLUB (SHCL)
Drenewydd, Park Hall, Oswestry SY11 4TB
The sleepy area of Park Hall, to the north-west of Oswestry, is home to a remarkable concentration of sports grounds including Oswestry Rugby Club, the dormant Oswestry Town's stadium, Shropshire County Showground and Oswestry Boys Club, new entrants in the County League. Drenewydd has two unrailed pitches and a modern clubhouse.

SHIFNAL UNITED (SHCL)
Idsall Sports Centre, Coppice Green Lane, Shifnal TF11 8PD
The Idsall Sports Centre is right next to Shifnal Town's Phoenix Park and is part of Idsall School. There are six pitches, the main one having a 'stake-and-tape' enclosure. Formerly used by Donnington Town.

SUTTON HILL (SHCL)
Bluebell Park, Sutton Hill, Telford TF7
Sutton Hill was one of the first parts of Telford New Town to be developed in the late 1960s. Bluebell Park is to the south of the main road into the estate, and has three pitches, one of which is railed off, all served by a brick pavilion. The ground has also been used in recent years by other County League clubs including Madeley Town, JFF Telford and St George's Town.

TELFORD JUNIORS (SHCL)
Ironbridge Power Station Sports Ground, Wenlock Road, Buildwas, Telford TF8 7BJ
Scenic ground dominated by the cooling towers of the power station, as seen in the photo below, although the sports ground is entirely separate. The main pitch is overlooked by a stylish 1970s pavilion with some overhang cover.

TIBBERTON UNITED/DAWLEY WANDERERS (SHCL)
Doseley Road, Dawley, Telford TF4 3AY
Basic ground next to Dawley by-pass. Has a post and rail barrier and a brick pavilion. Tibberton formerly used the Maslan Crescent Playing Fields in their home village a few miles north of Telford; this has a pair of dugouts which are gradually being taken over by advancing hedges.

WELLINGTON AMATEURS/JFF TELFORD (SHCL)
Grainger Drive, Leegomery, Telford TF1 6UL
Yet another multi-pitch complex in Telford New Town, Wellington's pitch has a post and rail surround as well as dugouts but no shelter.

WESTON RHYN (SHCL)
Recreation Ground, Weston Rhyn SY10 7RP
Coming from the A5, go right through the village until you come to a roundabout with a pub called The Lodge on the left. Turn left there and Weston Rhyn Recreation Ground is a little way down on the left. It has a permanent post and rail (as opposed to the stakes and ropes seen elsewhere), brick dug-outs and a smart white pavilion with a slate roof.

Gone But Not Forgotten
Armitage (c1970-1995)

Location: Kings Bromley Road, Handsacre, Armitage, Staffs.
Site now: Nature Field Study and Visitors Centre   Grid ref: SK095166

The village of Armitage had a football club from the early years of the 20th century when much of their time was spent in the Lichfield and District League. After reforming in 1946, Armitage joined the Staffordshire County League in 1952, moved up to the West Midlands League in 1971 and spent 13 years in the Premier Division after being promoted in 1974. In 1987 their third successive application for re-election was successful but three days before the start of the season Armitage decided to resign from the Premier Division and close down.

The club was reformed in 1990 as Armitage '90 and spent a season in the Staffordshire County League before joining the Midland Combination. In 1993 they were admitted to the Southern League as Midland Combination champions and with ambitious owners, it seemed that the club might climb even higher. However after two dreadful seasons in the Southern League, 1995 saw them drop back down to the Midland Football Alliance where they seemed to be recovering from this set-back as they led the league in December. It was then that the shock news came out that chairman Sid Osborn and chief executive Terry Brumpton were pulling out of the club to take over at Leicester United. As new owners could not be found in time, Armitage were forced to resign from the league and close down for the second time in only just over eight years. Less than a year later, Leicester United also closed down.

Above: Armitage's ground being put to an unusual use – bull storage. Taken by Dean Walton in December 1996. *Below*: A pitch roller left to rot as the forest takes hold (Jan 2001)

Until the early 1970s Armitage played on an undeveloped field in the village but then they moved almost two miles to the other side of the neighbouring village of Handsacre. The new ground was just off the Kings Bromley Road and soon provided cover for about 300 supporters and a small stand that initially claimed to seat 100, although this was later revised to 51. Floodlights appeared in 1979 and a new stand was erected in 1992 increasing the amount of seating to 300, while there was now covered accommodation for 500.

After the club finally closed, the ground was taken over by the Combined Handicapped and Disabled Society (CHADS) who turned the site into a nature field study and visitors centre for disabled and handicapped people. The buildings remain and are still recognisable but are now being used as offices and cover for equipment, while the pitch has been planted out with trees and shrubs.

Left: The stand put to use as a workshop (Feb 2003)

Brewood (c1902-2003)

Location: Engleton Lane, Brewood, Staffordshire
Site now: Still in use for Sunday football.

Grid ref: SJ888094

The Engleton Lane site has been used for cricket and football in the village since 1902 but it was not until ex-Wolves winger Terry Wharton became manager that Brewood F.C. began to spread its wings. In 1978 they left the Wolverhampton Amateur League for the West Midlands Regional League, where they won the Second Division in 1980 and the First in 1983. The club shared the changing rooms and clubhouse with the cricket club and added a small cover for 50 supporters and pitch surrounds, but this was still not enough to earn promotion to the Premier Division. Brewood continued in the WMRL until 1990 when after one season in the Staffordshire County League (South) they dropped down into Sunday football. The ground was sold by the football club to the village council who provided two pitches at right angles to the original, demolishing the cover and surround to achieve this. A new changing room block was built at the same time as the ground continues in use for Sunday football.

Below: The cover in 1994 (pic: Bob Lilliman)

Burton - Derby Turn (Burton Wanderers, 1871-1901)

Location: Derby Turn, Derby Road, Burton-on-Trent
Site now: Railway warehouse   Grid ref: SK248242

Burton Wanderers were formed in 1871 and spent their entire 30-year life at their Derby Turn ground with three of those years being as a reasonably successful - on the pitch - Football League club. Records of the ground are very sparse but it is believed to have occupied a field a short way along Derby Road from the Derby Turn Inn. There was a clubhouse at the ground and in 1892 the committee made a determined effort to improve facilities. Ash banks were built for standing and goal nets were used for the first time in Burton for Wanderers' Midland League game against Derby Junction on 1st October. A grandstand was opened in stages on the reserved side during the autumn with a temporary structure having been put in place until the permanent stand became available. The record crowd was established in 1894 when temporary extra stands had to be erected as 6,000 supporters saw Wanderers of the Midland League lose 2-1 at home to Notts County in the last 16 of the F.A. Cup.

At the end of that season a number of minor improvements were made to the ground to make it ready for entry to the Football League. These included new posts and ropes all around the pitch and improvements to the grandstand which now had a press stand in the centre. However Wanderers dropped out of the Football League in 1897 and at a low ebb both on the field and financially, they merged with Burton Swifts in 1901. The ground was sold to the Midland Railway who quickly extended their adjacent sidings and built a bonded warehouse and grain store which is still on the site today.

Burton - Peel Croft (Burton Swifts/United, 1890-1910)

Location: Peel Croft, Lichfield Street, Burton-on-Trent.
Site now: Home ground of Burton F.C. (Burton rugby club)   Grid ref: SK247224

Burton Swifts' early grounds included Burton cricket ground and Kidger's Field in Shobnall Street but in 1890 they moved in to the town's prime sporting venue of Peel Croft in Lichfield Street. There they remained until their demise in 1910, with the period between 1892 and 1907 spent in the Football League, the last six years as Burton United after the merger with Wanderers in 1901. Peel Croft was developed gradually during the club's Football League years with a main stand being built on the northern side, terracing on the opposite side and cover behind the western goal.

Right: Peel Croft's 1907 grandstand

1907 was a dreadful year for the club as the stand was destroyed by fire and a few weeks later the club was voted out of the League. However, the club found support from a local brewer called Eadie who contributed £300 to the £200 insurance money that the club received, thus allowing a new stand to be built.

Estimates of its seating capacity varied from 600 to 800 and it included a press box as well as dressing rooms and four bars underneath. United joined the Birmingham League but finished bottom in 1910 and their outstanding debts were probably a key factor in the League's decision not to re-elect them. Unable to pay the previous year's £70 rent for Peel Croft, the club became homeless, unable to start the season and thus defunct.

Burton rugby club quickly took over at Peel Croft and have remained there ever since with many of the developments undertaken by United still surviving today. The main stand on the north side is the one that was built in 1907 and the banking at the Lichfield Street still surviving today. The main stand on the north side is the one that was built in 1907 and the banking and have remained there ever since with many at the Lichfield Street end too is almost certainly unchanged. There is railway sleeper and ash terracing on the south side and although this has been covered in recent years, it is probably the same terracing that was in use from about 1901. Only at the west end are there no traces from a century ago as the cover has disappeared and been replaced by a simple walkway. Nevertheless, Peel Croft must be one of the best preserved old grounds in the country.

Right ground, wrong posts – Peel Croft has been home to Burton's rugby club since 1910.

Burton - The Crescent (Burton All Saints/Town, c1909-1939)

Location: The Crescent, Victoria Crescent, Burton-on-Trent.
Site now: The Carousels housing estate.
Grid ref: SK242244

Burton Town had joined the Burton and District League around 1902 as Burton All Saints and in 1907 they were playing in a field at the back of the Beehive pub in the High Street that would have been close to where the library now stands. They moved to the Crescent brewery ground in about 1909 and revived senior football in Burton in 1919 when they joined the Birmingham Combination. They soon began to develop the Crescent, providing

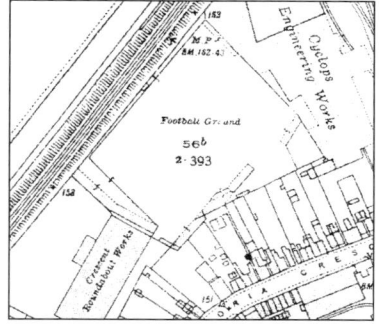

Above: *The Crescent ground on the 1937 O.S. map.*

banking on both sides and cover behind the goal at the southern end. Later a stand and additional cover was provided on the eastern side and there was also partial cover on the side opposite.

In 1931-32 and by now in the Birmingham League, they reached the third round of the F.A. Cup where they were drawn at home to First Division Blackburn Rovers. The Crescent ground was packed to the roof for this game with an official attendance of 9,674, the largest ever at a football match in Burton. Even this figure was supplemented by several hundreds who watched from the railway embankment alongside the ground and from empty railway wagons parked in the sidings. Burton lost 4-0 but continued as one of the strongest non-League clubs in the country until war broke out in 1939. However they were unable to reform when it finished six years later and although the Crescent remained as an open area for many years, it eventually succumbed to housing.

Below*: A magnificent view of The Crescent in 1935 (Aerofilms A47861)*

Burton - Wellington Street (Burton Albion, 1950-1958)

Location: Wellington Street, Burton-on-Trent.
Site now: Car park adjacent to the Burton Car Centre.   Grid ref: SK237228

Burton Albion's first ground after their formation in 1950 was the Lloyds Foundry sports ground in Wellington Street. The facilities were rather basic for such a prominent club, with covered terracing behind the eastern end but open terracing at the other end and along the northern side. There was a small stand on the southern side and the players had to change using Lloyds Foundry facilities in the factory behind that stand. The club had several crowds of more than 5,000 at Wellington Street but when they joined the Southern League in 1958, a ground with better facilities was needed and so they bought part of shoemakers Eatoughs' sports ground for £2,000 and named it Eton Park. The Wellington Street pitch remained in situ for a number of years but the site is now used for parking close to Burton Car Centre.

Cannock Town (c1900-1937)

Location: Brookfield Ground, Walsall Road, Bridgetown, Cannock.
Site now: Offices, formerly NCB Computer Centre.   Grid ref: SJ985095

The first Cannock Town dated from 1868 and used at least four different fields in the town before settling at what became known as the Brookfield Ground in Bridgtown. The club were founder members of the Walsall and District League in 1892 and joined the Birmingham Combination in 1909. In 1921 they were Combination champions and moved up to the Birmingham League where they spent the rest of their life apart from another 5-year spell in the Combination. In January 1937 their worsening financial position finally overtook them and they closed down in mid-season.

The Brookfield Ground had its entrance off the Walsall Road almost opposite the end of St. John's Road and was initially as undeveloped as all Cannock's previous fields. However when the club joined the Birmingham League "several hundred pounds" were found to provide substantial dressing rooms and soon afterwards a small wooden grandstand was built. Two years after the club's closure, war broke out and

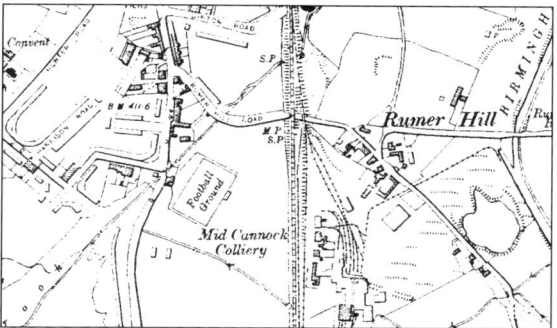

Above: *The Brookfield Ground on the 1938 O.S. map.*

the ground was covered with military buildings and used as a camp for the Polish Free Army. The site later became a miners' hostel until 1956 when the buildings were adopted as housing for Hungarian refugees following the uprising there. The buildings were used as offices when the National Coal Board took over the site in the early 1960s but they were eventually replaced as the NCB developed its own massive computer centre. Today the centre is owned by Atos Origin who provide a range of computer services through their Compower subsidiary.

The ground just shows up on this aerial photograph from 1930 (Aerofilms A34011)

Cannock Town (1991-1994)

Location: Littleton Miners Welfare Centre, Avon Road, Cannock.
Site now: Derelict, Waste Land. Grid ref: SJ979098

The Littleton Miners Welfare Sports Ground was first developed after the first world war, included a pavilion and was shared with Mid-Cannock Miners Welfare. It remained as a colliery sports ground until 1991 when a newly formed Cannock Town moved in and joined the Staffordshire County League (South). The club progressed rapidly and in 1993 they joined the Refuge Assurance Midland League. The ground was improved with refurbished changing rooms, a post and rail surround and three concrete dug-outs but the club only got the benefit of these improvements for a few months because early in 1994, their landlords British Coal closed down Littleton Colliery and with it, the Miners Welfare Centre. The club moved to Cannock Stadium to complete the season, but the costs of continuing there were prohibitive and so Cannock Town closed down after just a three year life. After the closure in 1994 the buildings were demolished and since then the land has been allowed to remain derelict.

Castlecroft (Wolverhampton Wanderers 'A', c1956-1982)

Location: Castlecroft Road, Wolverhampton
Site now: RFU Regional Centre Grid ref: SO873976

Castlecroft in Wolverhampton is as obscure a ground as they come, but not without significance. For a start, it was officially opened in 1956 by the most powerful man in British football – Sir Stanley Rous, then FA Secretary but later to become top dog at FIFA. Castlecroft was the training ground of Wolverhampton Wanderers, the most successful club of the 1950s, and at the time the development of the facility was every bit as progressive as the glamorous floodlit friendlies that made the club famous. The main pitch had a 500-seater Grandstand with a brick base and flat wooden roof, and was floodlit by bulbs mounted on ten quite elegant pylons. Wolves 'A' team played Birmingham League matches here against the likes of Burton and Nuneaton. It seems that the venue fell out of use in the early 1980s, when the Wanderers' financial struggles almost put them out of existence. The neighbouring Wolverhampton Rugby Club looked after the pitch until the Rugby Football Union itself took on the ground in the mid-1990s and turned it into the main Youth Development Centre for English Rugby. The old stand has been replaced

Above: Castlecroft's original stand, seen in 1990. **Below**: The impressive new stand built by the RFU.

by an impressive, elevated cantilever stand, which adjoins a substantial facilities and administration block. The floodlight pylons remain, although the bulbs are new.

Chasetown (c1958-1983)

Location: Burntwood Recreation Centre, High Street, Chase Terrace, Chasetown, Cannock.
Site now: Part of multi-use recreation centre.   Grid ref: SK048087

Formed in 1954 as Chase Terrace Old Scholars Youth Club, Chasetown played in local football until 1961 when they joined the Staffordshire County League (South). In 1972 they adopted their current title and moved up to the West Midlands League Division One where they immediately established themselves as one of the division's top sides. In the next 11 years they were champions of the division once and runners-up five times but were always denied promotion to the Premier Division due to the inadequacy of the facilities at their Burntwood Recreation Centre ground, even despite the existence of an impressive 300-seater stand on the site. However the problem was finally solved in 1983 when the stand was razed to the ground by a fire and the club was able to earn promotion by moving to a former council refuse tip and building a new ground which they christened The Scholars.

The Burntwood Recreation Centre ground was an open field until shortly after the second world war when the stand was erected as part of its development as the Cannock Chase Colliery Sports Ground. Both Cannock Chase Colliery F.C. and Chase Terrace United used the ground in those early post-war years when they were members of the Staffordshire County League. Cannock Chase Colliery left the league in 1958 but Chase Terrace United continued in it for many years until they disappeared in the 1970s after which Chasetown became the main occupants. After their move to the Scholars the site was gradually developed as a multi-use recreation centre and so the football pitch remains and may still see occasional use for either rugby or football. However since the disappearance of the stand, the only remaining facility is a post and rail on one side of the pitch while the area formerly occupied by the stand is now used for car parking.

Below: *An extremely rare view of the imposing grandstand at the Burntwood Recreation Centre, taken by Bob Lilliman in 1979. We have estimated seating capacity at 300, but the stand may well have been capable of holding more.*

Cheddleton Asylum (c1897-1970)

Location: St. Edward's Hospital, Cheddleton, Leek. Site now: A field. Grid ref: SJ974532

In 1897 a new Staffordshire County mental hospital was built on a site just north of Cheddleton. From the very first a high priority was given to the sports activities of the staff and so there were separate cricket and football pitches established in the spacious hospital grounds. Indeed in later years it was often said that new staff were recruited for the hospital based on their sporting abilities! By 1912 the Cheddleton Asylum football team was strong enough to join the North Staffordshire & District (later Staffordshire County) League, where they met such opposition as Port Vale reserves and Congleton Town. The team later changed name to Cheddleton Mental Hospital and remained members of the league for many years, their hey-day being in the 1920s - 30s when they were champions on more than one occasion.

At first the ground was just a marked-out pitch in a field but by the early 1930s the Hospital's maintenance staff had built a stand on either side. Each was roughly 50 feet long and positioned a few yards back from the touchlines, straddling the half-way line. The stands had solid wooden ends, a galvanised metal roof that sloped away from the pitch and although there were no seats, there were about five steps of terracing made from wooden railway sleepers.

The stand on the northern side, which was the nearer to the hospital, was for the use of hospital patients, while all other supporters used the southern side. Players had to change in the hospital buildings for many years but this was a few hundred yards from the pitch and changing rooms were provided behind the goal nearest the ground entrance in the 1950s.

By that time though, the team was on the decline and the ground was being used mostly by Cheddleton village teams, Cheddleton and Cheddleton United. Gradually even this usage declined and the by now dilapidated stands - which had remained virtually unaltered since their original construction - were dismantled, probably in the 1970s. Rugby posts were put up later and although these are still there, the ground is currently used just for grazing cattle.

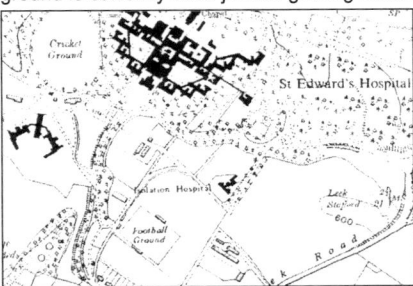

Above: The twin stands can be clearly seen on the 1955 OS map.

Below: Action at Cheddleton in the 1950s, with a tantalising glimpse of one of the home-built stands. Note also the relaxed posture of the player on the extreme right.

Cobridge Athletic Grounds (1886-1913)

Location: Waterloo Road, Cobridge, Stoke-on-Trent.
Site now: Playing fields and housing.   Grid ref: SJ874486

Port Vale played at a number of fields in their early days before moving to Moorland Road in Burslem in 1884 and adding Burslem as a prefix to their name. After two years they were forced to move again and so secured a 21-year lease on the Cobridge Athletic Grounds. This was an oval, multi-sport arena built on waste land and used for athletics, cycling and tennis as well as football. There was a pavilion on the south side of the ground but within a few years the club had built a brick grandstand at a cost of £200 that included a seating area and altogether accommodated 1,000 people. The pavilion was also replaced and further cover provided for supporters on the north side of the ground.

Vale joined the Football League in 1892 and remained there until 1907 with just a two year break back down in the Midland League between 1896 and 1898. However attendances were rarely good and the financial position of the club was therefore never very strong. By June 1907 things had become so desperate that a decision was made to wind the club up.

The ground was immediately taken over by a local junior team called Cobridge Church who renamed their first team "Port Vale". They played in local football for four years but still managed to attract crowds of up to 9,000 on occasions and so joined the Central League in 1911 where they quickly became successful. However in 1913 areas of the Cobridge Athletic Ground began to sink due to mining subsidence and so a group of Hanley businessmen took the opportunity to offer the club the use of the Hanley Recreation Ground.

Cobridge survived its subsidence problems and the accommodation was improved so that it was later home to greyhound racing and American Football and renamed the Cobridge Stadium. However this has now disappeared and the area is covered by housing and playing fields.

Right: Cobridge Athletic Grounds fell on a join in the 1899 OS map

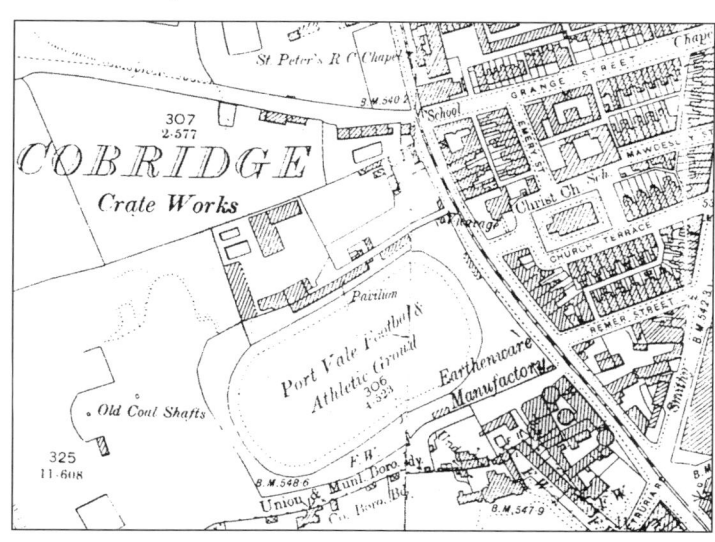

Eastwood (Hanley) (1946-1994) & Hanford (1982-1994)

Location: Berryhill Fields, Trentmill Road, Hanley, Stoke-on-Trent.
Site now: Buildings derelict, pitches used.
Grid ref: SJ893465 and SJ894466

Eastwood were formed in 1946 and played in local football before joining the Staffordshire County League (North) and moving up to the Mid-Cheshire League in 1965. They spent 1967-68 in the Manchester League and at the end of the season they became Eastwood (Hanley) to avoid confusion with Eastwood Town in Nottinghamshire. Also in 1968 they began a ten year spell in the West Midlands Regional League before moving to the Cheshire League in 1978 and the North-West Counties League in 1982.

The club's home was at Berryhill Fields in Trentmill Road where they leased two pitches from the National Coal Board. Initially there were just changing rooms on the site with the more northerly of the two pitches being used by Eastwood's reserves and also by Trent Rovers, a junior team who sub-leased the pitch. Eastwood's first team used the more southerly pitch and in the early 1970's built a stand on one side that provided cover for 500 and seating for 300 although this latter figure was later reduced to 100 as ground regulations altered. The ground's overall capacity was claimed to be 12,500 although the record crowd was just 5,500, established in 1978 when Stoke City played there in a benefit match. There was also a clubhouse but floodlights were not erected until 1986 when a team of Eastwood volunteers drove to Arbroath from where

they brought back the Gayfield Park floodlights before re-erecting them at Trentmill Road.

In 1982 Eastwood absorbed Trent Rovers and the adjacent pitch was then taken over by another junior club called Hanford who had been founded in 1959 as Hanford Boys Club. Hanford provided a basic cover for a few dozen spectators but the major developments were around Eastwood's pitch. In 1984 the stand was drastically rebuilt to meet new requirements and then seated 200 while the overall ground capacity was given as 5,000, of which 1,000 were under cover following installation of three steps of covered terracing stretching for approximately two-thirds of the length of the pitch on the side opposite to the stand. In 1988 the amount of covered accommodation was increased to 1,500 by roofing one end.

Above: Eastwood's grandstand circa 1990 (by Andy Dakin).
Right: Note the section to the right with the stanchions, which was still standing in 2002.

Eastwood had reached the Northern Premier League in 1987 and a new clubhouse was built in 1989 but the side dropped back into the North-West Counties League in 1990 and the isolated location of the site meant that it began to attract vandals. Two junior pitches on the other side of Trentmill Road were the first to suffer, then the Hanford ground and then the Eastwood ground itself. This culminated in arsonists burning down the dressing rooms in the summer of 1994 and so both Eastwood and Hanford were forced to leave Trentmill Road.

Hanford moved to their current home in the Northwood Stadium but Eastwood's status meant they needed a higher level of accommodation. They spent two years groundsharing with Kidsgrove Athletic and a year with Newcastle Town but the loss of clubhouse revenue hit them badly and in 1997 they had to give up the unequal struggle and disband. After the two clubs left Berryhill Fields, the facilities had to be abandoned to their fate and today lie derelict although both pitches remain in use for junior football.

Above: The overgrown side terrace contrasts with the neatly cut pitch (2002). **Below**: A rare view of the primitive cover on the neighbouring pitch used by Hanford (taken by Andy Dakin, circa 1990).

G.K.N. Sankey (1960-1988)

Location: Sankey Stadium, Castle Street, Hadley, Telford.
Site now: Structures disappeared, terracing and pitch overgrown.   Grid ref: SJ676122

The Sankey car components factory at Hadley Castle appeared in the early years of the century and the works football team was formed in 1910. The club first appeared in the Wellington League in 1911 under the title of Castle Works, became Hadley Castle Works after the first world war and Sankey's (Hadley) in 1953 playing on various fields within the large works complex. The 1950s and 1960s saw a huge boom in car ownership and the prosperity of the football club's parent company was reflected by the decision taken in 1960 to leave local football after 50 years and join the Cheshire League, then seen as one rung below the Football League. Probably to help non-locals find them, the club now became known as Sankey's (Wellington) and the five years in this league were under that title.

The enhanced status demanded enhanced facilities and an entirely new ground was produced for the club on company land next to Castle Street. An imposing 500-seater cantilever stand with dressing rooms and tea bars, etc. underneath was built on the south side and three rows of covered concrete terracing that could accommodate 1,000 spectators were constructed opposite it. The ends however were left as flat standing areas and the ground then remained virtually unchanged from the time it first appeared until it was demolished. Thus floodlights, which were rare at non-League level in 1960, were never installed. The overall capacity at the Sankey Stadium was 5,000 but the record attendance is believed to have been just 1,500, established in their first season in the Cheshire League when the novelty of having a new senior club in the area produced exceptional interest. The team spent 5 years in the Cheshire League and 20 in the West Midlands Regional League with two brief periods back in local football but despite their excellent facilities it is doubtful if the support they received was ever sufficient for them to pay their own way. As the British car industry declined, so the parent company's willingness to support the club also declined and in 1988 G.K.N. (who took over Sankey's in 1968) ceased their funding of the club, thereby bringing about its inevitable closure.

Above: A magnificent view of the Sankey Stadium in 1977 (Aerofilms A336119). The railway has now been grassed over and is a public path.

Above: The superb elevated stand, seen in 1977 (pic: Bob Lilliman). **Below**: The remains of the terracing on the railway side of the ground, now hidden behind a row of trees.

The ground remained in situ until about 1993 when the main stand was demolished and much of the steel structure of the terrace cover transported to Pelsall Villa's Bush ground where it was reassembled so that 500 seats could be installed under its shelter. Since then the Sankey site has been fenced around and just left to nature so that the base of the stand and the three rows of terracing can still be found, as long as you are prepared to fight your way through the now luxuriant undergrowth.

Harrisons (c1962-1990)

Location: Hazel Lane, Great Wyrley, Staffordshire.
Site now: Structures disappeared, pitch in use.   Grid ref: SJ996068

There was a Harrisons Colliery F.C. in 1936-37 who were probably the fore-runners to the post-war Harrisons F.C. who were active by 1950. The club then played in junior football for a number of years before progressing via the Staffordshire County League (South) to reach the West Midlands Regional League in 1982. They moved up from Division Two to the Premier Division by 1985 but in 1990 they lost most of their playing squad and were forced to revert to junior football.

In the early 1960s Harrisons managed to secure a 199 year lease for a ground on former open-cast mining land in Hazel Lane, Great Wyrley. They used a 'Portakabin'-type building to change in but upon joining the WMRL in 1982, a permanent changing block was built together with a small stand seating 100 on the side nearest Hazel Lane. Later, cover was provided for another 100 spectators on the opposite side and although ground capacity was estimated at 2,000, it is unlikely that this was ever tested, nor was it ever found necessary to install floodlights. Meanwhile, some years after Harrisons ground first appeared, Great Wyrley F.C. also took up residence in Hazel Lane with the entrance to their ground being directly opposite to that of Harrisons.

After Harrisons senior side resigned from the WMRL, the ground continued to stage football for youth teams and Sunday sides but being some distance from the actual social club, it also began to attract vandals. In the late 1990s most of the metal sheeting in the stands was stolen and so the structures had to be removed and a year or so later, vandals also broke up and stripped the roof of the changing block. This then had to be demolished and although the culprits were caught by the police, no action was taken against them. The open age teams now playing at the site use Great Wyrley's new changing rooms although there are hopes that a new temporary building may be put in place, as the pitches continue to be used by Harrisons Sunday side.

Harrisons down the years (all by Bob Lilliman). **Top**: *the small seated stand in 1984.* **Above**: *More cover on the south of the pitch, seen in 1988.* **Below**: *The same cover in 1993, looking much the worse for wear*

Hednesford Town - 'The Tins' (1880-1904)

Location: 'The Tins', Anglesey Street, Hednesford, Staffordshire.   Grid ref: SK000123
Site now: Health Centre and other buildings between Anglesey Street and Eskrett Street.

Hednesford Town were formed in 1880 by the merger of two local teams and established their headquarters at the Anglesey Hotel in Market Street. There was a large field behind the hotel which was the club's first ground and this was used until 1904 when a local councillor agreed to pay off the club's £40 debts provided they moved their headquarters to the Cross Keys.

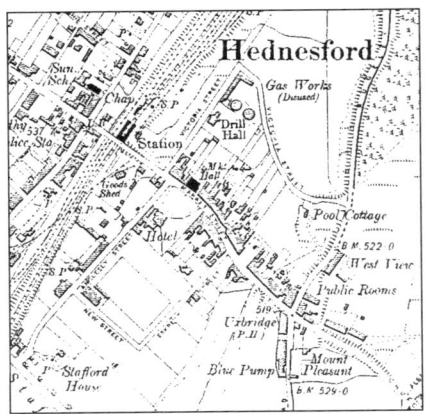

On this 1903 OS map, The Tins is the rectangular field in the bottom left corner.

The football pitch occupied the southern part of the field which was surrounded by tin sheeting about eight feet high hence the local name for the ground of 'The Tins'. The entrance was from the Anglesey Street end where there was an entrance hut and changing rooms - also constructed of tin sheeting - at the back of the hotel. The spectator facility consisted of a small lean-to shelter along the side of the pitch towards the Anglesey Street end which provided cover over about six or eight tiers of wooden terracing. The rest of the ground was simply an open field. The rudimentary stand disappeared piecemeal after Hednesford left the ground, as the materials were appropriated for use elsewhere but other fixtures found their way to the Cross Keys. The field itself survived until after the Second World War when it was quickly covered by a variety of buildings.

Hednesford Town - Cross Keys (1904-1995)

Location: Cross Keys, Hill Street, Hednesford, Staffordshire.
Site now: Housing, Keys Close and roads off it.   Grid ref: SK003114.

At the time of their move to a field behind the Cross Keys public house, Hednesford Town were playing in the Walsall and District League but in 1908 they moved up to the Birmingham Combination and so the ground was improved to accommodate the higher standard of football. The pitch was widened and turnstiles set up and it was at about the same time that a wooden stand was built on the northern side The exact date when this was built has not been found but it is known that it was after 1903 and before 1910. There was also ash banking around the ground at this time and

The cover at the pub end of the Cross Keys ground in 1979 (pic: Bob Lilliman). Note the old floodlights.

just after the first world war the overall capacity of Cross Keys was tested several times. In 1919 a new record of 6,000 was set in an F.A. Cup game against Walsall only for this to be raised to 7,000 a year later in another cup tie, against Willenhall. However both of these figures were put into the shade during Easter 1921 when a remarkable crowd of almost 10,000 attended the Birmingham League game against Walsall.

Above: The old main stand in 1979 (by Bob Lilliman) **Below**: The enlarged stand circa 1990 (by Andy Dakin) **Bottom**: The barn-like covered side terrace in 1979 (by Bob Lilliman)

However the large crowds soon disappeared and so Cross Keys remained basically unaltered for many years except for some cosmetic improvements undertaken in 1931 when the stand was re-painted and new pitch surrounds installed. In 1937 the posts and fences were moved to Cross Keys from the Anglesey Ground but it was not until 1948 that there were any significant changes. Then a steel framed cover with a corrugated roof was provided for up to 1,000 supporters at the Cross Keys end and cover was soon also provided on the side opposite to the stand. In 1953 the club was amongst the first to erect floodlights but this glory was short-lived as two years later a financial crisis precipitated their sale for £90 to Hednesford Hills Raceway where they were never erected. Another crisis was precipitated in November 1960 when the old main stand was blown down and although a temporary repair was effected, the stand was not properly rebuilt until 1963. In the 1970s the club once more began to improve the ground, putting up cover behind the eastern goal in 1971 and installing terracing on the old ash banks. The ground capacity was then estimated at 9,000 with cover for 2,000 and seating for just 200.

New floodlights were put up in 1981 and standing areas concreted two years later. Finally the old wooden stand - parts of which dated from before the first world war - was replaced in 1984, the new structure raising the seating accommodation to 350. At the same time Hednesford gained entry into the Southern League and with promotion to the Premier Division in 1992, the club's ambition was refuelled. Plans were made for a new ground but in the meantime, space was found to extend the seating at Cross Keys to 500. In 1995 and with immaculate timing, Hednesford won promotion to the Football Conference and were then able to leave Cross Keys and move to their new ground at Keys Park. Within a very short time, the 91-year-old ground was demolished and is now covered by housing, but the Cross Keys pub remains.

K Chell (1991-1994)

Location: Former Great Chell CC, Uplands Avenue, Chell, Tunstall, Stoke-on-Trent.
Site now: Buildings derelict, pitch now an open recreation area. Grid ref: SJ869530

Great Chell Cricket Club was once amongst the strongest in Staffordshire and in addition to a well-equipped pavilion, their ground at the end of Uplands Avenue provided open seating for 150 on one side of the ground and on the opposite side to this was a stand dating from the 1950s or early 1960s that provided cover for 1,500 on several rows of terracing. In the 1980s the ground was bought by local business man Graham Bailey and when in 1991 the cricket club decided to move on, Reg Barnsley - the former manager of Knypersley Victoria - formed a new football club and moved in. The new club christened itself K Chell and adapted the ground for football by installing hard standing, dug-outs and a post and rail around the pitch. The pavilion was re-fitted and converted into a two-tiered clubhouse and changing room complex, complete with a large car park, facilities for functions and capacity for over 200 people to watch matches from inside the building. The new clubhouse was known as Kay's Sports and Social Club after Mr. Bailey's wife Kay, hence also the 'K' in K Chell.

The massive changing and social club complex in 1993 (by Andy Dakin)

K Chell entered the West Midlands Regional League, won the Second Division championship at the first attempt and then transferred to the North-West Counties League at the request of the F.A. as they were considered too far north to compete in the southern half of the pyramid. This move to a much stronger league necessitated improvements to the former cricket ground and so almost 600 seats that had formerly been used at Vale Park were obtained and installed in the stand which was also refurbished. The hard standing was extended and the National Coal Board donated floodlight pylons which were fitted out with

A 1969 view of the then Great Chell Cricket Ground (Aerofilms A198635)

light bulbs that came from Leek Town although as they were never connected to the mains, their value was purely cosmetic!

Apart from this slight drawback, K Chell now had excellent facilities and also the space to expand should they progress further up the pyramid. However during their second season in Division Two of the NWCL, Mr. Bailey decided that he wanted to use the ground for a housing development and so in the summer of 1994, K Chell were forced to disband.

The housing development has not come about due to restrictions on use of the land and so this once well-equipped ground now lies sadly abandoned and has inevitably suffered at the hands of vandals. The former club-house was subject to at least one arson attack and has now been demolished while the once imposing stand has lost all its back panels and now stands as a forlorn and dejected relic overlooking a wilderness of vegetation that was once the pitch. What a tragic waste of a once superb facility.

Below 1: *The seated stand in 1993 (by Andy Dakin). Note the post and rail, dugouts and the floodlights that never worked.*
Below 2: *Just the shell remains in this view from 2002, the back panels having been knocked out.*
Left & top: *Two more views of one of the most evocative wrecked stadiums in English football.*

Ludlow Town (1981-2001)

Location: The Riddings, Riddings Road, Ludlow, Shropshire.
Site now: Housing development, Riddings Park.   Grid ref: SO523749

During their long history, Ludlow Town have played at a number of venues in the town with the MEB sports ground being their home immediately prior to 1981. The only building there though was a dressing room with an overhang and Ludlow's first developed football ground was The Riddings which they moved into prior to the start of the 1981-82 season. Initially this ground had as little in the way of spectator facilities as their previous grounds but there was soon a small clubhouse and in 1992 a cover was erected over three steps of concrete terracing, allowing up to 150 supporters to remain dry in bad weather.

The club had joined the West Midlands Regional League in 1978 but on at least one occasion had been denied promotion to the Premier Division due to their lack of floodlights. This was corrected in 1994 when the formation of the Midland Alliance created a number of vacancies in the top flight of the WMRL and Ludlow took advantage of the situation by at last installing lights and making the step up. The Riddings was further brought into line with grading requirements by the installation of around 60 seats under the existing cover while the terracing was extended from one end of the cover almost to the end of the pitch. The ground capacity was then estimated at 1,000 but the limitations of The Riddings were proving to be a handicap to the club's ambitions and in 1999 they unveiled plans for a new ground in the town. The club's chosen location was ruled out but a helpful council worked with them to identify a suitable site and Ludlow were then able to sell The Riddings which was quickly covered by housing. For two years the club were forced to ground-share at Blakenall and Shifnal but in 2003 they returned home with the opening of the brand new Coors Stadium.

Two views of Riddings Park in April 2001, weeks before Town left the ground for two years of exile.

Oakengates Town (1920-1938)

Location: The Charlton Arms Ground, Bridge Street, Oakengates, Shropshire.
Site now: Housing, Innes Avenue. Grid ref: SJ693108

There were football clubs in Oakengates at least as early as 1883 and a junior club called Oakengates Town was in existence between 1911 and 1914 but it was not until 1920 that the town had its first senior team. In that year a new limited company was set up to run a semi-professional team who were immediately accepted into the Birmingham Combination. Part of an unsightly pit mound near to the back of the Charlton Arms pub was turned into a presentable playing surface and before long changing rooms were built at the southern end of the ground and a grandstand with bench seats provided on the west side. Ash banking surrounded most of the rest of the ground. In 1923 the club were champions of the Birmingham Combination and moved up to the Birmingham League where their best season was in 1930-31 when defeat at Stafford in their last game meant that they missed the league title only on goal average. Consolation was gained in the Shropshire Senior Cup final when they lifted the cup after beating Shrewsbury Town 8-1!

The club's success prompted its management to improve further the Charlton ground. Additional cover was erected on the popular side and the reserved side opposite was also improved. Oakengates had another good season in 1931-32 but then the town began to suffer from business depression and the football club was soon in financial difficulties. In 1938 they decided to resign from the Birmingham League as it no longer provided local opposition, and were hit by a £50 fine that proved to be the last straw. The club was therefore put on ice for 12 months but with war imminent, it was never resurrected. Although it soon lost its buildings, the Charlton Ground survived as a football ground until the 1960s when it finally succumbed to housing development.

Above: *The Charlton ground shows up well on this 1926 OS map, as does the pit mound which dominates the extremely rare photograph of the ground (**below**, courtsey of Shropshire Libraries). Thought to have been taken in the early 1930s, the ground is just visible in the top-left corner, with the grandstand prominent.*

Oswestry Town - Victoria Road (c1879-1988)

Location: Victoria Road, Oswestry
Site now: Housing, Victoria Fields.
Grid ref: SJ294291

Oswestry F.C. was established at the Victoria Road cricket ground by 1879 and was never far away from the top of the non-League game for very long having played in the Welsh, Cheshire and Southern Leagues and, between 1979 and 1988, the Northern Premier League.

The first building at Victoria Road was the pavilion in the north-west corner but during the Second World War the eastern part of the ground was requisitioned for munitions and after that the football club had the ground to themselves. The ground developed principally down the western side with a wooden stand seating 500 being positioned towards the Victoria Road end. The rest of the western side was taken up by terracing, with a short open area next to the stand and cover for 1,000 to the southern end. The end behind the southern goal was open for many years but in the early 1980s this was also covered so that about 2,000 out of the total ground capacity of 5,500 could then be protected from the elements. The eastern side and northern end were uncovered open areas apart from the entrances and clubhouse which were situated behind the northern goal while eight pylons provided floodlighting for Victoria Road. In the aftermath of the 1985 Bradford fire, the old wooden stand was deemed unsafe by the local authorities and so had to be demolished and replaced with modern structure that seated 350.

By 1987 Oswestry's debts were

Victoria Road on the day of its last game, versus Mossley in the NPL on 2nd April 1988.
Above: The main stand and covered terrace on the west side. **Below**: The abandoned southern end of the ground was already derelict.
Bottom: A view to the social club and entrance, with two more areas of cover.

substantial and there was no alternative but to sell Victoria Road in order to pay them off and to find a new home. The club had identified a site near to the Park Hall Stadium where they hoped to develop a new ground but found

that this plan was blocked by the existence of a covenant that prevented its use for sport. The Park Hall Stadium itself was home to the local hockey team who were also approached but no agreement could be reached. A number of ground-shares were investigated but again these were unsatisfactory for one reason or another and so at the end of the 1987-88 season the club found itself homeless, unable to continue playing and thus became dormant. The Victoria Road ground was quickly demolished and replaced with housing although the recently built stand was dismantled and stored in the hope that it could be re-erected elsewhere.

Oswestry Town - Park Hall Stadium (1993-2003)

Location: Park Hall Stadium, Burma Road, Park Hall, Oswestry.   Grid Ref: SJ310315
Site now: Continues in use for junior football.

In the event it was five years before Oswestry Town took the field again when they opted to join the Welsh pyramid. Despite the club's former status they had to start at a rather humble level in the Welsh National League (Wrexham Area) but progressed well, reaching the top of the pyramid in 2000 with promotion to the League of Wales. This rebirth had eventually come about because of a new requirement that hockey pitches had to have artificial surfaces, causing the local hockey club to vacate the Park Hall Stadium and allowing Oswestry Town to move in. The stadium had formerly been part of an army National Service Centre and included a running track surrounded by considerable banking that gave excellent views. In 1968 the local council had built a stand, allowing spectators to sit under cover on concrete steps. The football club quickly set to work to adapt Park Hall for football and installed the seats from Victoria Road in the stand. This seating was later extended by using seats from Telford United's old Buck's Head ground and the shop and tea bar came from the same source. The Victoria Road stand was not re-erected though and so presumably remains in store.

Oswestry struggled in the League of Wales while at the same time and despite their considerable financial backing, the aspirations of nearby TNS Llansantffraid were being limited by their remote village location. In the summer of 2003 TNS and Oswestry therefore agreed a merger which would see TNS move to Oswestry in around 2005 where the improved access would help their ambitions in Europe, always assuming that UEFA and the Welsh FA will agree to a club based in England being the Welsh representatives. At present TNS continue to play in Llansantffraid while Park Hall hosts their reserves and ladies' teams as once again the Oswestry Town name has disappeared. Hopefully the merger will be allowed and an attractive new football stadium will appear in Oswestry to benefit the whole community.

Two views of the Park Hall Stadium, set in woodland to the north-east of Oswestry.

St. George's (Wellington)

Location: Church Street Recreation Ground, St. George's, Oakengates.
Site now: St. George's Cricket Club.   Grid ref: SJ711109

The St.George's club who were members of the Birmingham League between the wars was the third from the village to attain senior status. The first St. George's had a proud record of achievement but disbanded in February 1900 while members of the Birmingham League. The second had started life as Trench Victoria, moved to St. George's in 1902 and became St. George's Victoria. They had three seasons in the Birmingham Combination but in 1912 they too disbanded.

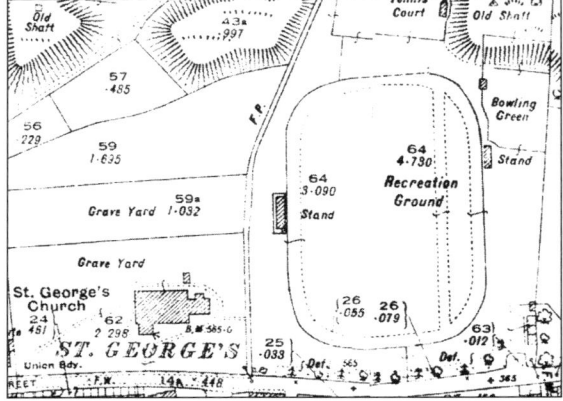

After the war the third major club called St. George's were formed and in 1922 became members of the Birmingham Combination. Knocking Tranmere Rovers out of the F.A. Cup helped them to gain a place in the Birmingham League in 1924 but after seven seasons they were voted out and gradually subsided into junior football.

The first two St. George's clubs played on an undeveloped field in Church Street known as the Vicarage Field however the later club took up residence instead on the recreation ground

Above: *The unusual St George's ground on the 1926 OS map. Note the sprint track cutting across the oval. The 'Finish Line Grandstand' is also visible on the right, and this is pictured **below** during the 1923 annual St George's Sports (courtesy Jim Cooper).*

which was the next field to the west and right next to the church. This ground had been established in 1902 as a cycling and athletics venue with a banked and fenced oval circuit which in later years included a water jump for steeplechasers. There was also a separate 100 yard sprint track on the side farthest from the

church with a quoits mound near to it. A grandstand that straddled what became the football club's halfway line was built on the side nearest the church. This stand had a solid metal frame with corrugated panels and wooden bench seats and probably seated around 200. Later a second, smaller stand of less solid construction was erected on the opposite side, near to the finish of the sprint track. Its main purpose was for spectators to be able to watch the sprints and quoits but it also gave reasonable views of the football beyond. St. George's attendance figures in the Birmingham League were respectable, particularly if they were playing a local derby against Wellington (now Telford United), Shrewsbury or Oakengates but the best crowd at the Church Street Recreation Ground was almost certainly the 6,000 who watched the 1922 F.A. Cup tie against Walsall. This figure was rarely challenged although in 1924, 5,000 spectators watched the Midland A.A.A. championships and were privileged to witness the legendary Harold Abrahams win three events just a few weeks before he won a gold medal in the 100 yards at the Paris Olympics.

After St. George's dropped out of the Birmingham League in 1931, cricket became the dominant game at Church Street. The cricketers had been playing on the old Vicarage Field (which can be seen behind the stand in the view taken from the church tower) but they soon expanded their ground towards the recreation ground, demolishing the smaller - and newer - stand to do so. The main stand though survived into the 1960s and was only finally removed when the cricketers took over the old football ground, swapping pitches with the by now, junior footballers. The situation remains the same today, with the recreation ground used for St. George's and occasionally Shropshire cricket clubs, while the former cricket pitch is now used for both the summer and winter games.

Two fine views of the Church Street Rec. **Above**: This shot from the church tower, taken by Len Grice in 1930, shows the sprint track on the far side of the field, and the Vicarage Field beyond the 'Finish Line Stand'. **Below**: A much later view towards the church, with the original grandstand in full view (Shropshire Records & Research/Jim Cooper).

Shifnal Town (1979-1985)

Location: Admiral's Park, Drayton Road, Shifnal.
Site now: Housing, Admiral's Way. Grid ref: SJ753085

There have been a number of Shifnal Town clubs, the first having been formed in 1877 and playing regular games with Aston Villa and Wolverhampton Wanderers but recent clubs have had a more modest fixture list. The present Shifnal Town was formed in 1964 as St. Andrew's Youth Club and played at the Idsall School Sports Centre in the Wellington League and Shropshire County League. They changed their name to Shifnal Town and joined the West Midlands League in 1976, winning promotion to the Premier Division three years later.

Shifnal then leased a piece of land at the former Admiral's Farm from Bridgnorth Council and established their Admiral's Park ground there. Volunteers built dressing rooms and in 1981 acover that provided shelter on the southern side for 200 standing supporters. A new clubhouse followed in 1983 as the club went from strength to strength. There was an overall claimed capacity of 5,000 at the ground but this was never remotely tested, the record of 1,002 being established in 1983-84 when Bridgnorth Town were the visitors in the F.A. Vase. The club were champions of the WMRL Premier Division in both 1981 and 1982 but were unable to claim promotion to the Southern League through lack of floodlights at the ground. In 1986 and despite Shifnal's success, the council decided to use the land for housing and so the club were forced to drop back down to County League football at the Idsall Sports Centre. They were on the verge of disbanding altogether but after seven years of hard work at this lower level, the Shifnal committee were finally able to establish a fine new ground at nearby Phoenix Park where their future should now be assured.

Below: The cover at Admiral's Park lasted just four seasons, so pictures of it are pretty rare. Luckily for us, Bob Lilliman took this picture in 1984.

Star (Bridgnorth) (1964-2002)

Location: Stourbridge Road, Bridgnorth.
Site now: Vacated ready for factory extension. Grid ref: SO729920

The works football team of the Star Aluminium company in Bridgnorth was formed in 1964. They played in the Bridgnorth and Kidderminster Leagues before graduating from the Shropshire County League to the West Midlands Regional League in 1997 and then being promoted to the WMRL Premier Division in their first season.

Ever since formation the team played on a pitch at the back of the works which had plenty of room for expansion. The ground remained undeveloped until 1998 when promotion to the WMRL Premier Division resulted in a small metal stand with a curved roof being built on the southern side of the pitch. This accommodated a total of 78 supporters in four tiers of tip-up seats. Hard standing was laid down along that side and behind both goals, floodlights were erected and soon afterwards a second stand was constructed opposite the first. This was wooden and had eight rows of seats that provided covered accommodation for a further 100 spectators. There were also a pair of substantial dug-outs on both sides of the pitch, with one pair being used for players and the other for club officials.

However in 2002 came the bombshell that the club's parent company wanted to use the football pitch for a factory expansion. Faced with the alternative of risking workers' jobs, Star had no choice but to acquiesce in the decision and so moved back down to the Shropshire County League for the 2002-03 season. They were able to use the ground until November but then had to play the rest of their games away from home. At the end of the season, Star were put on ice until a new ground could be found with both the parent company and the local council assisting with the search. At the time of writing the ground is gradually disappearing, with the floodlights dismantled and the wooden stand demolished

Above: The older of the two stands at Star
Below: Incredibly, this wooden stand was built after the metal stand. **_Bottom_**: A general view with the factory in the background, taken in early 2003.

and although the metal stand and its pair of officials' dug-outs are still extant, they have now lost their seats.

NON-LEAGUE GROUNDS ● 79 ● STAFFORDSHIRE & SHROPSHIRE

Tamworth Castle - Castle Pleasure Grounds (1913-1925)

Location: Tamworth Castle Pleasure Grounds.
Site now: Open grassed area   Grid ref: SK209036

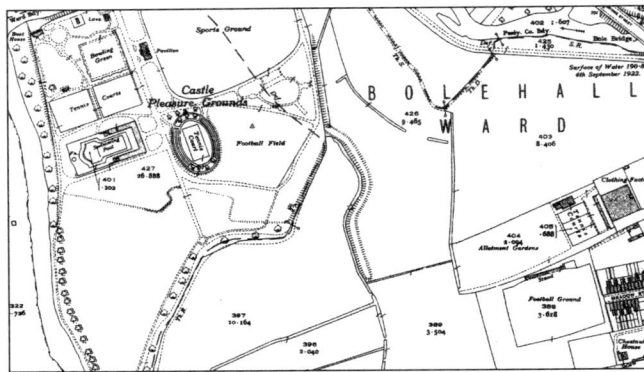

The first Tamworth club to achieve senior status was Tamworth Castle, who joined the Birmingham Combination in 1913 and also had two years in the Birmingham League before disbanding in 1928. During this period they played most of their home games on the Castle Pleasure Grounds, a huge recreational area just south of the town and used an inn in Market Street called the Town Hall Vaults for changing. The ground was situated in what today is the open grass area between the tennis courts and Anker Drive but had no facilities for spectators other than some low banking behind one goal. In 1925 the newly formed Tamworth Rugby Club took over the lease from the council while Tamworth Castle moved to a ground behind the Jolly Sailor Inn. From then on, the Pleasure Grounds pitch was used principally for rugby although Mile Oak Rovers were based on a second pitch in the grounds from their foundation in 1958 until 1960. The fascinating 1938 OS map above shows the layout of the Castle Pleasure Fields in the top left, and also the fledgling Lamb Ground in the bottom right corner. The famous 'Egg' roundabout was eventually built in the space between the two grounds.

Tamworth Castle/Tamworth - Jolly Sailor Ground (1925-1934)

Location: Jolly Sailor Inn, Fazeley Road, Tamworth.
Site now: Housing and River Drive   Grid ref: SK205035

The Jolly Sailor ground was part of extensive leisure facilities attached to the inn and had been used since at least 1902. By 1925 its limited development consisted of a post and wire enclosure and some raised ash banks. It was situated close to the back of the pub and is now partly covered by housing and partly by River Drive. After the demise of Tamworth Castle it also became the first home of the present Tamworth club who were formed in 1933. Tamworth leased the ground at a cost of 10s. (50p) per match and supporters spent considerable effort to refurbish it, with banking being built up for more than half the length of the pitch. However after one season there, the landlord at the Jolly Sailor wished to treble the rent to 30s. (£1.50) and so the club came to an agreement instead to use the Lamb field, where the rent was the same as the club had been paying for the Jolly Sailor. There was a worry that crowds would decrease compared to the popular Jolly Sailor, but these proved unfounded and the Lamb has now been the club's home for almost 70 years.

Telford United - (Old) Buck's Head Ground (c1890-2000)

Location: The (Old) Buck's Head, Watling Street, Wellington.
Site now: The (New) Buck's Head   Grid ref: SJ663112

Wellington Town came into being in 1879 when the previous Wellington Parish Church Institute club reformed under that name. The new club's first ground was at Eyton but after a season there, they moved to Haygate where they stayed until 1886. Two seasons at Street Lane followed before another move, this time to a field at the back of the rather remote Admaston Spa hotel. The move to the Buck's Head field came in about 1890 which makes the ground the oldest in Shropshire, it already having been used by other clubs since at least 1885.

There were soon wooden changing rooms at the Watling Street end of the ground and by 1912 a small stand had been built. This also had wooden frames and cross pieces with a corrugated tin roof and sides. Most of the rest of the pitch was surrounded by banking. In March 1935 it was agreed to erect a covered stand to seat 1,000 spectators on the Western side at an estimated cost of £1,000 and this was opened in September of the same year. The record crowd at the Buck's Head was established later that season when an official attendance of 11,836 watched the Good Friday game against Shrewsbury Town in the Shropshire Cup. By that time there was already a cover at the back of the western side although facilities on that side were always limited by the complete lack of services such as water and electricity.

The banking was terraced in stages although not all areas were ever dealt with and in 1948

Buck's Head in 1969. The pub which lends its name to the ground is on the far right by the junction, and is the only remaining reference point at the new ground (Aerofilms A198450).

NON-LEAGUE GROUNDS ● 81 ● STAFFORDSHIRE & SHROPSHIRE

much work was needed at the Regent Street (northern) end as a brook had to be piped in before the terrace there and its cover could be erected. The ground was further improved in 1949 when 10 feet of soil were removed from the Buck's Head end in order to level the pitch and at about the same time, new dressing rooms were opened beneath the stand. The ground became floodlit in March 1965 at a cost of £10,000 but soon afterwards the club's financial problems meant that they had to seek assistance from Telford Development Corporation who were controlling the regeneration of the area as a new town. In 1969 the club changed its name to Telford United and in November of that year plans for the redevelopment of the ground were formulated. June 1970 saw the formation of a Telford United new stadium committee and in 1973 the Corporation finally bought the ground for £55,000 with a condition that allowed the club to buy it back for the same price as and when they could afford it. Almost immediately after the sale, work started on a new East Stand which was completed in April 1974 at a cost of £35,000 and seated 920. It was used for a Shropshire Senior Cup game at the end of the season but was officially opened in August 1974 by Sir Stanley Rous. However the positioning

and design of this stand left something to be desired as it was simply perched in the middle of the East terrace and cut off the view of large parts of the pitch for many people on the terraces on either side of it.

In December 1980 Telford put forward plans to turn the Buck's Head into a 29,000 capacity stadium but this was turned down by the council who said that Telford Town Park would be a more suitable location. The club rejected that idea and so the Buck's Head remained largely unchanged although it was still good enough to be awarded an "A" grade, i.e. suitable for the Football League, in June 1982. Telford has long maintained a position near to the top of the non-League pyramid and for many years has harboured the ambition to move up to the Football League. In 1998 Miras Leisure Whitehouse Hotels became major shareholders in the club and they have provided the necessary backing which should allow Telford to fulfil its undoubted potential. This backing has allowed the old Buck's Head to be levelled and replaced by a superb new stadium that is probably the best in non-League football (see p. 16).

Top: The 1974 East Stand seen in 1979 before Maxell advertising was plastered across the fascia (pic: Bob Lilliman).
Left: The West Stand circa 1990 (pic: Andy Dakin).

More Gone But Not Forgotten Grounds

Albrighton United re-formed in 1946 and played on the Malt House Field in Station Road (SJ815042), changing at the infants school across the road. In 1959 the Malt House itself burned down but the field was used until 1964 with the players frequently training in the blackened shell of the former brewery building. The ground was then used to build the Fairlawns housing estate so the club moved out of the village to a farm field at Little Harriet's Hayes (SJ835048). In 1970 they moved to a new ground at the Clockmills (SJ804046) with purpose built changing rooms and in 1977 they entered the West Midlands League where they remained for six years. The intention was to move to a better positioned ground situated in Loak Road (SJ803045) which was only a goal-kick away from the Clockmills, but just as this became available in 1983, the club collapsed amidst allegations of financial mismanagement. A new club called **Albrighton Sports and Social** was formed and played in the Shropshire County League for a while before moving to Sunday football. The Clockmills ground now lies abandoned while the beautifully kept Loak Road ground is used for youth football.

The Clockmills ground in Albrighton (by Bob Lilliman)

Bandon were formed in 1988 as a pub team from the Bandon Arms. They played on a few different fields in Bridgnorth until 1994 when they moved to a pitch in Bandon Lane (SO721933), which was off Mill Lane and close to the river. They moved up from the Kidderminster League to the West Midlands Regional League in 1995 and were promoted to the Premier Division in 1998 but despite finishing 4th in 1999-2000, they were forced to disband in the close season. The club had developed the Bandon Lane ground with a post and rail pitch surround and also with slabs and gravel to provide hard standing along the northern side where they erected a small, primitive cover consisting of a 15 x 8 foot tin roof supported by four poles. Despite being regularly flooded by the nearby Severn, the pitch drained well and was once used just two weeks after lying under six feet of water. However the team's success outpaced their ability to improve the ground and in 1997 they were forced to leave and share Bridgnorth Town's floodlit Crown Meadow. They remained there until May 2000 when they were unable to find £10,000 needed to fund their costs for the next season and with Bridgnorth wishing to use Crown Meadow for their reserves, Bandon became homeless. A local businessman attempted a last minute rescue but the WMRL decreed that having resigned from the league, Bandon had forfeited their place in the Premier Division and would have to start again in Division One. The club decided instead to disband but the Bandon Lane ground survives, now being used for youth football.

Brownhills Town were formed in about 1980 and initially played on a clay-type surface at the youth club where the football club was started. This pitch became unacceptable to opponents as the team moved up to better leagues and after playing at a local school and at the cricket ground by The Parade, in 1990 they moved out of Brownhills itself and across the county border into Staffordshire and on to a ground in Hanney Hay Road on the outskirts of Hammerwich (SK058069). This ground though was very basic with just dug-outs, a post and rail pitch surround and pre-fabricated concrete changing rooms. As there was no mains electricity connected to the site, the club also had to rely on a small generator for power. With the ground being earmarked as part of the route for the new Birmingham North Relief Road motorway, the club had some leverage that helped them to move back into Brownhills in 1996. Meanwhile the Hanney Hay Road ground is now under tarmac, awaiting the speeding vehicles of millions of drivers who would otherwise be fuming in the car park that is sometimes misleadingly referred to as the M6 motorway.

Donnington Wood date back to 1910 but played principally in local football before joining Division One of the West Midlands Regional League in 1976. They maintained good positions in the table until 1983 when they suffered the indignity of enforced relegation for failing to fulfil a fixture. At the time the club were playing at the Bell in Donnington which was simply an open recreation ground but after regaining their First Division place in 1987 they moved to Duke Street at Donnington Wood (SJ707112). This was a properly enclosed ground with changing rooms close by the entrance, dug-outs on one side of the pitch and a small cover opposite. Hard standing was laid down for a short distance in front of this cover and also in front of the dug-outs and there was a post and rail pitch surround. However mining subsidence was a continual problem with holes appearing from time to time and in 1993 the council decided to fill these in properly and sell the ground for housing. Donnington Wood moved to the New Road ground of the junior Wrockwardine Wood club but in 1994 they were forced to resign from the WMRL due to the league's rule that changing rooms had to be in the confines of the ground whereas at New Road, they were located within the adjacent leisure centre. The Charity Commission vetoed the proposed improvements and so the club effectively folded. Wrockwardine Wood continued at New Road at a junior level with a rump of Donnington Wood members joining them and in 2001 Wrockwardine Wood themselves were able to join the WMRL.

Donnington Wood in 1993 (pic: Brian Cook)

Dresden United were formed in the early 1880s and played on a ground in Cocknage Road (SJ911421), almost certainly the open area opposite the eastern end of Queens Park. Dresden played in both The Combination and the Midland League between 1892 and 1897 where their opponents included Wrexham, Stockport County, Walsall and Barnsley. The club's results were reasonably good but the costs of running a team in the Midland League crippled them financially and after dropping back down to The Combination in 1897 they were forced to resign from the league in January 1898. A junior team called Dresden took over the Cocknage Road ground and Dresden Queens Park also played there in the North Staffs League before WW1. Despite the senior level reached by Dresden United, no evidence has appeared that shows that they ever provided any spectator accommodation. Theground was later used for cricket, then for junior football again in the 1950s and finally rugby in the 1960s. However it is now covered by the housing of Barnes Way.

The **English Electric** works at Stafford grew between the wars to become one of the area's largest employers. A large area between the works and the railway was used as the company's sports field and the football pitch - which even had a small grandstand - was roughly south-east of the factory. The continuing success of the business meant that factory expansions gradually took over more of the sports field and the grandstand disappeared either during the war or soon after it as the football pitch was moved to different areas. In 1990 the pitch moved again to an area west of the works known as The Hough which had formerly been used for cricket and in 1993 another move was made to what became the final location, close to the railway line (SJ928220). By that time the company had become part of the **GEC** group while the works team had played in both north and south sections of the Staffs County League. They moved up to the Staffordshire Senior League in 1994 and although there was a plan to install floodlights at about the same time, lack of finance meant that this never happened. In 1997 the connection with the social club was broken and the GEC name disappeared although the manager and squad continued in Sunday football at Weston as **Woolpack FC**. At present the final football pitch survives as an open grass area.

Above: *The works and sports ground of English Electric in 1930. (Aerofilms A34011)*

Florence Colliery ran a miners' football team from the early years of the century and they were champions of the North Staffordshire Federation in 1908 when the league included Port Vale's first team who were on their long way back to the Football League. After the Second World War Florence were regular members of the Staffordshire County League (North) and for many years their ground (SJ913418) was sandwiched between the colliery itself and the railway branch line that served it. The approach to the ground was from Cocknage Road and past the changing rooms which were the only facility and were also used for the adjacent cricket pitch. In the 1960s the railway lines expanded over both grounds and so the club were forced to retreat to the other side of the pit next to the Lightwood Road. The pit and its railwaylines have now disappeared and the site of the old ground is covered by the housing of Durham Drive.

Ironbridge were one of Shropshire's strongest clubs in the last years of the 19th century. They were founder members of the Birmingham League in 1889, three times champions of the Shropshire League and four times winners of the Shropshire Senior Cup. They were also twice semi-finalists in the Birmingham Senior Cup in the days when West Bromwich Albion, Aston Villa and the likes fielded their first teams in the competition. Indeed it was in the Birmingham Senior Cup of 1889-90 that Ironbridge attracted a crowd of 3,000 for the visit of Villa's first team to the Hill Top ground (SJ687040). Although the club played at this venue at a senior level for around 20 years, no evidence has been found that there was ever a stand or other permanent accommodation for spectators. The club declined after the turn of the century but Hill Top continued to be used by junior clubs in Ironbridge until the 1950s when it was covered by the Glendinning Housing Estate.

Abbey Green Road in Leek

The first **Leek F.C.** changed from rugby to football in January 1877 when their home was at Bridge End (SJ974573). This ground must have been very close to or even on the same site as the current Harrison Park but only a month after changing codes, Leek moved to the Old Recreation Ground (SJ982565), which was where Gladstone Street now stands. After just a few weeks another move was made to a more permanent address in Westwood Lane, now Westwood Street (SJ975565) and in the summer of 1884 the club bought an old railway carriage for use as dressing rooms there. This would have been used by the celebrated Glasgow side Queens Park before they beat Leek 3-2 in front of a 3,000 crowd in the last 32 of the F.A. Cup on January 3rd 1885. That same season Leek erected a grandstand at the ground and in 1886 they attracted a record crowd of 5,000 a respectable figure for a town of 14,000, but a decline in Leek's fortunes saw the crowds begin to dwindle. The club left Westwood Lane in 1888 and after brief stays at other fields in the town, they settled at Broad's Bridge in Abbey Green Road (SJ978573). Housing quickly covered the Westwood Lane ground but the Abbey Green Road site is still in use as a junior football ground. Indeed this was also home to **Leek County School Old Boys** from around 1980 after they left the Birchall playing fields until they moved in with Leek Town in 1991. However despite its long history, the only facilities at Abbey Green Road have been changing rooms and a post and rail pitch surround.

Two grounds in Lichfield have briefly seen senior football although neither had any substantial spectator facilities. The Barn Field (SK118088) was the home of **Lichfield City United** who moved in c1910 as Lichfield Phoenix and played in the Birmingham Combination from 1923 to 1925. There was a sentry style pay box and a post and wire pitch surround but players had to change in one of the nearby pubs. After the club disbanded for financial reasons in 1925, the ground continued in use for junior football until the 1970s when it was covered by housing.

Shortbutts Lane (SK118084) was the home ground of **Lichfield F.C.** from 1970 and saw West Midlands Regional League football from 1976. However as it is a public recreation ground, the club were unable to erect floodlights or develop it in any way and they also suffered from vandalism.

They therefore left in 1992 and arranged groundshares elsewhere but four years later and with no prospect of a return to the city, they disbanded and reverted to Sunday football. The pitch is still used at Shortbutts Lane but the changing room block from the WMRL days has been demolished.

Penkridge Town were playing at the Monckton Recreation Ground (SJ918139) from soon after the Second World War. The ground had dug-outs and a small cover for standing supporters and also a pitch surround of concrete posts and steel rails. The cover disappeared in the 1970s with the other fixtures gradually following but the club stayed there until vandalism meant that it became too difficult to keep up the standard of maintenance.

Penkridge felt that they would be unable to progress from the Staffordshire County League through the pyramid if they remained at the Monckton and so they moved a mile or so from the village centre to Rodbaston Agricultural College. The Monckton Recreation Ground is still there with the football pitch remaining as part of an open area.

Shortbutts Lane in Lichfield (by Bob Lilliman)

Rists United are another works club who reached county league level. Founded in 1956, they played in the Newcastle and District League and moved up from the Staffordshire County League (North) to the Staffordshire Senior League in 1991. The works club ground was in Lower Milehouse Lane (SJ837477) where some minimal cover was available. However the side has now withdrawn from senior football and the former ground is just a field, its buildings having disappeared.

Football began in Shrewsbury in the 1860s and there were soon several teams in the town. One of the most important grounds used was the Racecourse at Monkmoor (SJ505128) which was used by **Shrewsbury F.C.** who disappeared in 1879 and also by **Shropshire Wanderers** during their run through to the F.A. Cup semi-finals in 1874-75. The present **Shrewsbury Town** used the Racecourse immediately after their formation in 1886 but the grandstand was too distant from the pitch for use for football and in 1889 the rental cost of the ground persuaded Shrewsbury to move across what is now Monkmoor Road to Ambler's Field (SJ504129). The club transferred to a ground in Sutton Lane in 1893 and in 1895 they moved to the Barracks Ground in Copthorne Road (SJ481127). The Sutton Lane ground was probably the field (SJ498115) near to the engine sheds that was almost completely surrounded by railway lines. It is now a set of allotments at the end of Lavender Way. No evidence has been found of any spectator accommodation at either Ambler's Field or Sutton Lane but a small grandstand was erected at the Barracks Ground not many years before Shrewsbury left for the Gay Meadow in 1910. Both Ambler's Field and the Barracks Ground are now covered by housing; Underdale Avenue and Bradford Street stand on Ambler's Field and Copthorne Drive on the Barracks Ground. Racing ceased at the racecourse shortly after the first world war and it was used as an airfield for a while before it too became used for housing. Street names of Racecourse Avenue, Racecourse Crescent and Racecourse Green give the merest hint of their ancestry.

After the disappearance of the first Shrewsbury F.C., there was another, short-lived **Shrewsbury Town**. This Shrewsbury Town were formed in 1881 principally by old boys of Shrewsbury School who re-formed **Shropshire Wanderers** at the same time. The clubs arranged impressive fixture lists and together set up a new ground in Cemetery Road (SJ490112). The 1881-82 Shropshire Cup final was played on this new

Rists United (by Bob Lilliman)

ground but after just a year's activity, both clubs disappeared and **Shrewsbury Trinity** used Cemetery Road for a while before the ground fell into disuse. Nevertheless the field still survives with an unusual barn dating from the 1930s standing in one corner on the spot where the original pavilion is believed to have been erected. Cemetery Road itself is now known as Drawell Street.

It is also worth mentioning the Comet Field at Ditherington (SJ502140). From 1880 to 1885 this was home to **Shrewsbury Castle Blues** who were Shrewsbury's leading club of the period but were also well known for their violent play. In 1885 the Comet Field was taken over by **Shrewsbury Castle Rovers** and in January 1886 they met Wellington Town there in a Shropshire Cup match. Some Castle Blues players were amongst the crowd and they joined the players of Castle Rovers both during and after the game in administering a series of kickings and beatings to the Wellington team. As a result both Shrewsbury clubs had to disband at the end of the season as no one else was prepared to play them. Shrewsbury badly needed a new club to restore the town's tarnished football image and so it was that the present **Shrewsbury Town** was formed in May 1886. The Comet Field's reputation seems to have suffered at the same time and it was much less used after the infamous brawl. It is now covered by an industrial estate.

The Silkmore Lane ground of Staffs Police (by Bob Lilliman)

The **Staffordshire Police** team were formed in 1953, graduated to the Staffordshire County League (North) in 1982 and also played for several years in the Staffordshire Senior League. The police sports ground was situated in Silkmore Lane, Stafford (SJ935214) and in addition to the changing rooms, it boasted a post and rail on one side together with a small cover. The ground is no longer used and the buildings have disappeared but the post and rail survives while the pitch is still in reasonable condition. However it seems that it will not be long before this too succumbs to a housing development.

For many years the Staffordshire County Cricket Ground (SJ880458) was located almost opposite the main entrance to Stoke railway station and in the closing years of the 19th century it was also used occasionally for football. A number of representative games were played there with the first probably being the England international trial on 18th December 1886 between the Amateurs and the Professionals. **Stoke** (now Stoke City) played their Football Alliance fixture against Crewe Alexandra there on November 8th 1890 when the Victoria Ground was flooded and in the same season the ground was also home to **Staffs County**, who were founder members of The Combination. Staffs County though failed to complete the season and after this the use of the ground for football seems to have quickly declined. Apart from the pavilion, it is thought that there was some early provision for spectators at the County Cricket Ground which survived for cricket until the 1950s although it is now part of the local university campus.

The first club in **Whitchurch** was formed as early as 1865 and although other fields in the town were used for time to time and the club had at least one re-formation, their usual home from the very earliest days was at the cricket ground in Talbot Street (SJ549418). In 1923 - when they were two years into a 12-year membership of the Cheshire League - they moved just around the corner from Talbot Street to Yockings Park. The Talbot Street cricket ground's only accommodation was the pavilion in the western corner and the ground disappeared in the 1930s when it was covered by the housing of Talbot Crescent.

Wrockwardine United have the surprising claim of being the first club in Shropshire to put up floodlights. The team was based in the village of Wrockwardine, just west of Wellington and had no connection with Wrockwardine Wood F.C.. Wrockwardine United was founded straight after the war when instead of celebrating the return of their men-folk by collecting money for a party, the villagers raised enough funds to secure tenancy of the local football field. The players bought a disused RAF building from High Ercall for a changing room and in the early 1950s they erected floodlights with bulbs of the ordinary screw in type. However the installation was not an immediate success as the very first game under the new lights had to be abandoned when it began to rain soon after the start and all the light-bulbs blew. The lights were later used successfully but there was never a great need for them and they were probably taken down after just one season. The club were highly successful in the Wellington League and graduated to the Shropshire County League in 1956 but lasted in that for just one season and later disappeared completely. The lights and changing rooms were the only facilities at the ground which is now a farm field (SJ623126), although the dilapidated changing rooms can still be seen in the corner.

The big switch-on at Wrockwardine United. Floodlighting has come a long way in half a century (Picture courtesy of Partnership Publishing).

The Drawing Board

This little section is devoted to grounds that 'could have been' or 'still might be', but they all exist only on the drawing board.

With Telford United safely installed in their magnificently rebuilt stadium, all three of their Conference rivals covered in this book are also hoping to build brand new grounds that are suitable for the Football League. Shrewsbury hope to move to a 10,000 all-seater stadium at Oteley Road near Meole Brace, Burton Albion's plan is to use the Pirelli site opposite Eton Park for a 6,000 capacity ground of which 2,000 will be seated while Tamworth hope to move to a 7,000 all-seater off Dunstall Lane at Bitterscote.

All three had stated that they hoped to be in their new grounds by the start of the 2004-05 season but such moves are notoriously difficult to accomplish. Shrewsbury have planning permission for the new ground but the move is dependent on a suitable development of the Gay Meadow. The plan to build apartments on the site has now been replaced with plans for a theatre and it seems that the Gay Meadow will continue to be the club's home for at least another year or two. Similarly, with the new location of Tamworth's ground still to be agreed with the local authorities, they will still be at the Lamb until at least 2005.

At the other end of the scale, Penkridge Town hope to shortly develop a modest new ground within the confines of Rodbaston Agricultural College, and the fact that Tamworth-based junior club Coton Green's most senior side plays in Division 8 of the Birmingham AFA hasn't stopped them obtaining £334,000 from the Football Foundation to develop facilities on the old Fazeley Swifts ground in New Mill Lane, Tamworth.

The difficulty in moving to a new ground is

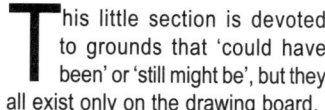

TAMWORTH'S £45,000 SPORTS ARENA

not however a recent phenomenon. In 1947 Tamworth had plans for a new 15,000 capacity stadium to be built at a cost of £45,000 in the Castle Pleasure Grounds (see contemporary artist's impression above, from the *Tamworth Herald*). The stadium would have been a multi-sports arena requiring the ground level to be raised by more than two metres to overcome the risk of flooding but enthusiasm waned as costs rose and the project was shelved. In the last 15 years Burton Albion have also looked around for a new ground on more than one occasion while in 1980 Telford United's own development plans for the Buck's Head were rejected by the new town development corporation who wanted them to move to a ground in the town park.

In the early 1990s Lichfield pinned all their hopes for the future on a new ground they hoped to build on Christian Fields. Like the Tamworth project nearly 50 years earlier this was to be a multi-sport stadium but as the site was a former rubbish tip, it was found that it would be several years before it could be declared clear of methane gas. With no prospect of a return to their home city in the foreseeable future, Lichfield joined the long line of clubs forced out of senior football due to their inability to find a suitable new ground.

Grounds Around the Borders

As you travel round the landlocked counties of Staffordshire and Shropshire, it would be a shame to miss out on some of the notable grounds that lie just over the borders, so this section aims to highlight the best of these, starting in South Shropshire.

Tenbury United's neat Palmer's Meadow ground lies just inside Worcestershire in the town of Tenbury Wells, and is staging West Midlands League football for the first time in 2003/04. There is no cover but the ground has a quaint fence and post pitch surround. Driving west through Herefordshire ultimately takes you into Wales and the Bryn-y-Castell ground of **Knighton Town**, separated from England by the Teme Valley. Formerly in the Cymru Alliance, Knighton are now in the Mid-Wales League (South) and their ground has a cosy stand capable of seating about 100.

Further north, a mile or so west of where Offa's Dyke Path forms the border with England, lies the Clos-tan-y-mur ground of **Montgomery**. This is really an open field, but there is a fair-sized stand framed by a lovely view of the town and surrounding hills. Rather good for the Montgomeryshire League. A few miles north is Berriew, where the Recreation Ground plays host to the Mid-Wales League games of **Berriew AFC**. The ground has a small stand positioned in front of the clubhouse.

Welshpool is one of the more strategic towns in Mid-Wales, and there are notable grounds belonging to Waterloo Rovers, Welshpool Town and Guilsfield. Taking the A458 back towards England, however, brings you through the long village of Trewern. Hidden behind the school on the main road is the ground used by Montgomeryshire Leaguers **Trewern United**, complete with a tall, rusting covered terrace which was once painted sky blue. If you hadn't been told about this ground you would be very unlikely to come across it by chance, and yet it is the very essence of that old cliché, the hidden gem.

Bestriding the Mid-Wales football scene, and for that matter the entire League of Wales are **Total Network Solutions**, the full-time professional side based a couple of miles inside the border at Llansantffraid. Their home, the Treflan Recreation Ground, has been much improved and can seat 500 under cover in two

Welsh delights: <u>Top</u>: Knighton Town **Above**: Montgomery FC **Below**: Trewern United **Bottom**: TNS Llansantffraid, LoW Champions

stands, but the owner of TNS has much bigger ambitions for the club, and has eyed Oswestry as the ideal place for a purpose built stadium. As a first step, Oswestry Town have agreed to a merger with TNS (see page 75), but Treflan is likely to be used for a few seasons to come.

Back in England, Cheshire club **Alsager Town**'s natural local derby would be against Kidsgrove if they were in the same division. Alsager have made huge improvements to their Town Ground in Wood Park in order to progress to Division One of the North-West Counties League. Set in a slight hollow, the ground has two sections of cover set below the clubhouse. Alsager's actual derby is now against **Congleton Town**, whose ground in Booth Street has a very 'Northern' feel to it, being perched on a hill in the middle of a housing estate. The grandstand is a modern cantilever replacing a rather more characterful 1920s stand. Grass banking at the top end of the ground provides a precarious but worthwhile view.

Due east of Stoke, the **Ashbourne Recreation Ground** is less than two miles into Derbyshire from the border. Quite why **Ashbourne United**, the town's leading club, chooses to play 8 miles away at Rocester is a mystery, as the Rec is a charming venue with a small cover and a scenic backdrop.

Further south in Derbyshire, the Hawfields ground of Midland Combination club **Newhall United** occupies a surprisingly large site in the middle of this tightly packed town just to the east of Burton. The rambling ground has two sections of cover and is a splendid antidote to antiseptic modern grounds. In Tamworth, two notable grounds fall just inside Warwickshire, each borne out of the mining industry. **Birch Coppice Colliery** play on a fine ground on the A5 in Dordon, and possess a 50-yard cover which has unfortunately lost its roof. **Polesworth North Warwick** play on another former welfare ground at Hermitage Hill, this one having a cover behind one goal. Last on our tour of the fringes is Abbey Park, home of former Southern Leaguers **Bloxwich Town**. Although I have not put this to the test, I am sure that with the aid of a step ladder and a pair of binoculars, you could watch a game here from Staffordshire.

Top: Alsager Town **Above**: Congleton Town **Below**: Ashbourne Rec.

Index

Abbey Hulton United 49
Adderley Green 31
Albrighton S & S 83
Albrighton United 83
Alsagers Bank 49
Alsager Town 91
Arbroath 64
Armitage 54
Ashbourne United 33, 91
Audley & District 40
Ball Haye Green 40
Bandon 83
Belle Vue OB 52
Belvidere Colts 51
Berriew 90
Biddulph Victoria 18, 43
Bilbrook 49
Birch Coppice Colliery 91
Bishop's Castle 51
Bloxwich Town 91
Bolehall Swifts 19
Brereton Social 41
Brewood 55
Bridgnorth Town 20, 83
Bristol City 5
Brocton 21, 46, 49
Broseley Athletic 51
Broseley Colts 51
Broseley Juniors 51
Brown Clee 51
Brownhills Town 83
Burntwood Town 41
Burslem Port Vale 63
Burton Albion 4, 58, 89
Burton All Saints 57
Burton RFC 45
Burton Swifts 56
Burton Town 57
Burton United 56
Burton Wanderers 56
Cannock Chase FC 50
Cannock Chase Colliery 61
Cannock Stadium 2, 21, 60
Cannock Town 59, 60
Castlecroft (Ground) 60
Chase Terrace OS 61
Chase Terrace United 61
Chasetown 22, 61
Cheadle Town OB 49
Cheddleton 62
Cheddleton Asylum/MH 62
Cheddleton United 62
Church Stretton Town 51
Clee Hill United 51
Cobridge Church 63
Congleton Town 91
Coton Green 89
Craven Arms Town 51
Dawley Wanderers 53
Denver 27
Donnington Town 53
Donnington Wood 84
Drayton Town 28, 51
Dresden Queens Park 84
Dresden United 84

Dudley United LFC 23
Eastwood (Hanley) 24, 64
Eccleshall 42
Ellesmere Rangers 52
English Electric 84
Enville Athletic 49
Fazeley Swifts 89
Featherstone Prison 39, 49
Florence (Colliery) 42, 85
Foley 3, 43
Four Ashes 49
GEC Stafford 84
GKN Sankey 65
Goldenhill Wanderers 43
Great Chell CC 70
Great Wyrley 44, 67
Guilsfield 90
Handrahan Timbers 23
Hanford 24, 64
Hanley Town 44
Hanwood United 52
Harrisons 44, 67
Haughmond 52
Heath Hayes 25
Hednesford Progressive 50
Hednesford Town 6, 41, 50, 68
Highley Welfare 52
Holditch MW 49
Holt JCB 50
Hopesgate United 52
Ironbridge 85
JFF Telford 53
K Chell 70
Keys FC 50
Kidsgrove Athletic 26, 65
Knighton Town 90
Knypersley Victoria 18
Leek (FC) 86
Leek CSOB 8, 86
Leek Town 8, 71, 86
Leicester United 54
Leoni AG 31
Lichfield (City) 86, 89
Lichfield City United 86
Lilleshall 46
Little Drayton Rangers 28
Littleton MW 60
Ludlow Town 27, 72
Madeley Town 53
Manor Inne 43
Market Drayton Town 28, 51
Marston Wolves 51
Meir KA 36
Meole Brace 52
Mile Oak Rovers 45, 80
Milton Rangers/Utd 29
Montgomery 90
Morda United 45
Newcastle (on-Clun) 52
Newcastle Town 30, 50, 65
Newhall United 91
Newport Town 53
Northwich Victoria 26
Norton AG 31
Norton United 31

Oakengates Town 53, 73
Oswestry Boys Club 53
Oswestry Town 74, 75, 91
Parkway Clayton 50
Pelsall Villa 66
Penkridge Town 50, 86, 89
Polesworth NW 91
Port Vale 47, 63, 70
RAF Cosford 32
Redgate Clayton 50
Richard Thomas & Baldwins 23
Rising Brook 46
Rists United 87
Riverway 50
Rocester 33
Rowley Park (Stafford) 21, 46
Rugby Town 8
St George's (Wellington) 76
St George's Town 53
Sankey's (Wellington) 65
Shawbury United 37
Shenstone Pathfinder 50
Shifnal Town 34, 78
Shifnal United 53
Shrewsbury (FC) 87
Shrewsbury Castle Blues 87
Shrewsbury Castle Rovers 87
Shrewsbury Town 10, 27, 87, 89
Shrewsbury Trinity 87
Shropshire Wanderers 87
Sikh Hunters 44
Snailbeach White Star 52
Stafford Rangers 12, 46
Stafford Town 46
Staffordshire Police 88
Staffs County 88
Stallington 50
Stapenhill 35
Star (Bridgnorth) 78

Stoke (City) 64, 88
Stone Dominoes 1, 36, 47
Stone Old Alleynians 47
Sutton Hill 53
Tamworth 14, 80, 89
Tamworth Castle 45, 80
Telford Athletics Stadium 47, 48
Telford Juniors 53
Telford United 16, 75, 81, 89
Tenbury United 90
Tibberton United 53
Total Network Solutions 75, 90
Trench Victoria 76
Trent Rovers 64
Trewern United 90
Vale Juniors 43
Vale Victoria 18, 43
Waterloo Rovers 90
Wedgwood 50
Wellington Amateurs 53
Wellington Town 81
Welshpool Town 90
Wem Town 37
West Cannock Colliery 50
Weston Rhyn 53
Whitchurch 88
Whitchurch Alport 38
White Horse Rangers 47
Winding Wheel 50
Wolstanton United 50
Wolverhampton Casuals 39, 53
Wolverhampton Wanderers 32, 60
Woolpack FC 85
Worcester City 16
Wrockwardine United 88
Wrockwardine Wood 48, 84
Wyrley Rangers 51
Yates Club 48

Telford's West Stand in 1979 (Bob Lilliman)

Yates Club (October 2003)